Beyond the Bac

I0019500

A Comprehensive Guide to Frontend Development with Elixir

Zion Edwin

Table of Contents

Preface   4

Chapter 1: Introduction   7
   1.1 Why Elixir for the Frontend?   7
   1.2 The Modern Frontend Landscape   10
   1.3 Setting Up Your Development Environment   13

Chapter 2: HTML and CSS Fundamentals   17
   2.1 Building Blocks of the Web: HTML   17
   2.2 Styling with CSS   21
   2.3 Responsive Design   27
   2.4 Accessibility Considerations   31

Chapter 3: Introduction to JavaScript   35
   3.1 JavaScript Basics   35
   3.2 DOM Manipulation   41
   3.3 Working with APIs   46
   3.4 Modern JavaScript (ES6+)   50

Chapter 4: Phoenix Framework Fundamentals   56
   4.1 MVC Architecture in Phoenix   56
   4.2 Routing and Request Handling   60
   4.3 Working with Ecto   64
   4.4 Authentication and Authorization   68

Chapter 5: Introduction to LiveView   73
   5.1 The LiveView Philosophy   73
   5.2 Building Your First LiveView   77
   5.3 LiveView Lifecycle   81
   5.4 Forms and User Input   86

Chapter 6: Advanced LiveView Techniques   92
   6.1 Live Components: 92
   6.2 Live Navigation: 96
   6.3 Testing LiveViews   101
   6.4 Optimizing LiveView Performance   104

Chapter 7: JavaScript Interoperability   110
   7.1 Calling JavaScript from Elixir   110
   7.2 Calling Elixir from JavaScript   114
   7.3 Building LiveView Components with JavaScript   119

Chapter 8: Integrating Frontend Frameworks   **124**

8.1 Using JavaScript Libraries   124

8.2 Building Hybrid Applications   129

Chapter 9: Real-time Communication   **135**

9.1 Channels and Presence   135

9.2 WebSockets and Phoenix PubSub   143

Chapter 10: Case Study: Building a Real-Time Dashboard   **149**

10.1 Project Setup and Planning   150

10.2 Implementing Live Charts and Graphs   153

10.3 Integrating with External APIs   158

Chapter 11: Building an Interactive Game   **163**

11.1 Game Design and Logic   163

11.2 Handling User Input and Game State   166

11.3 Creating Animations and Visual Effects   171

Chapter 12: Deployment and Beyond   176

12.1 Deploying Phoenix Applications   176

12.2 Continuous Integration and Delivery   181

12.3 Performance Monitoring and Optimization   185

Conclusion   **189**

Preface

Fellow Elixir enthusiast! If you're reading this, chances are you've already fallen in love with Elixir's elegance and power for building robust and scalable backend systems. But let's be honest, sometimes the frontend can feel like a bit of a... *different* beast. Maybe you've dabbled in JavaScript, wrestled with CSS, or even felt a twinge of frustration trying to make your web applications truly shine.

Well, I've got some good news: you don't have to be a frontend wizard to create amazing user experiences with Elixir! This book is your friendly guide to venturing beyond the backend and mastering the art of frontend development with the Phoenix framework and its incredible LiveView technology.

Background and Motivation

When I first started working with Elixir, I was blown away by its concurrency, fault-tolerance, and the sheer joy of writing clean, functional code. But as my projects grew, I found myself yearning for a more streamlined and enjoyable way to build interactive user interfaces. That's when I discovered LiveView, and it completely changed my perspective on frontend development.

LiveView lets you build dynamic, real-time UIs with the same Elixir code you already know and love. No more context switching between languages, no more wrestling with complex client-side frameworks. It's a game-changer, and I'm incredibly excited to share its power with you.

Purpose and Scope

This book is designed to be your comprehensive companion on the path to frontend mastery with Elixir. We'll start with the fundamentals of HTML, CSS, and JavaScript, laying a solid foundation for building any web application. Then, we'll explore the Phoenix framework and dive headfirst into the magic of LiveView. You'll learn how to build everything from simple interactive elements to complex, real-time applications.

We'll also cover essential topics like JavaScript interoperability, integrating frontend frameworks, and real-time communication with Phoenix Channels. By the end of this book, you'll have the skills and confidence to create captivating, dynamic, and user-friendly web experiences with Elixir.

Target Audience

This book is perfect for you if:

- You're an Elixir developer who wants to expand your skills to include frontend development.
- You're familiar with Phoenix and want to learn how to build real-time UIs with LiveView.
- You're curious about frontend development but intimidated by the complexity of JavaScript frameworks.
- You're eager to create engaging and interactive web applications with the elegance and power of Elixir.

Organization and Structure

This book is structured to guide you through a clear and logical progression. We'll start with the basics, building up your knowledge step by step. Each chapter introduces new concepts, provides practical examples, and offers opportunities for you to practice and experiment.

Invitation to Read

So, grab your favorite beverage, fire up your code editor, and get ready to embark on an exciting adventure in frontend development with Elixir. I can't wait to show you what's possible!

Chapter 1: Introduction

Let's kick things off! You've cracked open this book, which means you're ready to take your Elixir skills to the next level. It's time to break free from the backend and explore the exciting world of frontend development with Elixir.

1.1 Why Elixir for the Frontend?

Elixir has gained a strong reputation for building robust and scalable backend systems. But you might be surprised to learn that Elixir is increasingly being used for frontend development as well. This is largely thanks to Phoenix, a web framework built in Elixir, and its innovative LiveView feature. Let's explore why Elixir is becoming a compelling choice for frontend development.

LiveView:

At the core of Elixir's frontend capabilities is LiveView. LiveView allows you to build dynamic, interactive user interfaces with server-rendered HTML. This means that instead of writing your frontend logic in JavaScript, you can use Elixir.

Here's how it works:

1. **Initial Page Load:** When a user visits your web page, the server renders the initial HTML and sends it to the browser.
2. **WebSocket Connection:** LiveView establishes a persistent connection between the browser and the server using WebSockets.

3. **Server-Side Updates:** When a user interacts with the page (e.g., clicks a button, submits a form), the event is sent to the server over the WebSocket connection.
4. **State Changes and Re-rendering:** The server processes the event, updates the application's state, and re-renders the necessary parts of the HTML.
5. **DOM Patching:** LiveView sends only the changed parts of the HTML to the browser, where they are efficiently patched into the existing page.

This approach provides a seamless and efficient way to build real-time user interfaces without writing extensive JavaScript code.

Benefits of Using Elixir for the Frontend

- **Reduced Complexity:** LiveView simplifies frontend development by allowing you to write both frontend and backend code in Elixir. This eliminates the need to switch between languages and frameworks, reducing cognitive overhead and potential errors.
- **Real-time Capabilities:** Elixir, built on the Erlang virtual machine (BEAM), excels at handling concurrent connections. This makes it ideal for building applications with real-time features like chat, collaborative tools, and live dashboards.
- **Increased Productivity:** LiveView often requires less code to achieve the same functionality as traditional JavaScript frameworks. This can lead to faster development cycles and improved maintainability.
- **Improved Performance:** By handling most of the logic on the server, LiveView can optimize

performance, especially for applications with complex user interactions.

- **Maintainability:** Elixir's functional nature and emphasis on immutability promote code that is easier to understand, test, and maintain, which is essential for managing complex frontend applications.

Key Concepts

- **WebSocket:** A communication protocol that provides a persistent, bidirectional connection between a web browser and a server. This allows for real-time data exchange.
- **Server-Side Rendering:** The process of generating HTML on the server and sending it to the browser. This is in contrast to client-side rendering, where JavaScript is used to generate HTML in the browser.
- **DOM (Document Object Model):** A programming interface for HTML and XML documents. It represents the page as a tree-like structure, allowing you to access and manipulate elements.
- **DOM Patching:** The process of updating only the changed parts of a web page, rather than re-rendering the entire page. This improves performance and reduces data transfer.

By combining the power of Elixir with the innovative approach of LiveView, you can create dynamic, real-time web applications with exceptional performance and maintainability.

1.2 The Modern Frontend Landscape

The frontend landscape of web development is constantly evolving, with new technologies and frameworks emerging regularly. However, the core principles remain rooted in three fundamental technologies: HTML, CSS, and JavaScript. Understanding these building blocks is crucial for anyone working in frontend development, even when using powerful tools like Elixir and LiveView.

HTML (HyperText Markup Language)

HTML is the backbone of every web page. It provides the structure and semantic meaning to the content. Think of it as the skeleton that defines the different parts of a web page, such as headings, paragraphs, images, and links.

- **Elements:** HTML uses elements to define the structure. Elements are represented by tags enclosed in angle brackets (e.g., <h1>, <p>, <img>).
- **Attributes:** Attributes provide additional information about HTML elements (e.g., src for images, href for links).
- **Semantic HTML:** This involves using HTML elements for their intended purpose, making the code more readable and accessible. For example, using <article> for blog posts, <nav> for navigation menus, and <aside> for sidebars.

CSS (Cascading Style Sheets)

CSS is the language used to style the presentation of web pages. It controls the visual aspects, such as colors, fonts, layout, and responsiveness.

- **Selectors:** Selectors are used to target specific HTML elements for styling. They can be based on element names, classes, IDs, and more.
- **Properties and Values:** CSS properties define the styling aspects (e.g., color, font-size, margin), and values specify the settings for those properties (e.g., blue, 16px, 10px).
- **Box Model:** Every HTML element is treated as a box with content, padding, border, and margin. Understanding the box model is essential for controlling the layout and spacing of elements.
- **Flexbox and Grid:** These are powerful layout tools in CSS that provide flexible ways to arrange elements on a page, making it easier to create responsive designs.

JavaScript

JavaScript is the programming language that brings interactivity to web pages. It allows developers to handle user input, manipulate the page dynamically, and make asynchronous requests to servers.

- **DOM (Document Object Model):** JavaScript interacts with the HTML document through the DOM. The DOM represents the page as a tree-like structure, allowing you to access and modify elements, attributes, and content.
- **Event Handling:** JavaScript can respond to user actions like clicks, mouseovers, and form submissions by attaching event listeners to elements.
- **Asynchronous JavaScript:** This allows JavaScript to perform tasks in the background without blocking the main thread, improving the user experience.

Techniques like AJAX (Asynchronous JavaScript and XML) and the Fetch API enable communication with servers without page reloads.

The Evolving Landscape

The frontend landscape is constantly evolving with new tools and frameworks. Here are some key trends:

- **Component-Based Architecture:** This approach involves breaking down user interfaces into reusable components, making code more organized and maintainable. Popular JavaScript frameworks like React, Vue, and Angular embrace this paradigm.
- **Single-Page Applications (SPAs):** SPAs load a single HTML page and dynamically update content as the user interacts with the[1] application, providing a more fluid and app-like experience.
- **Progressive Web Apps (PWAs):** PWAs combine the best of web and mobile apps, offering features like offline access, push notifications, and installability.

While this book focuses on Elixir and LiveView for frontend development, having a basic understanding of these core technologies and trends is valuable for any web developer. It allows you to appreciate the broader context and make informed decisions when building your applications.

1.3 Setting Up Your Development Environment

Before we start building amazing things with Elixir and LiveView, we need to prepare your computer for development. This involves installing the necessary tools and configuring your system. Don't worry, this setup process is straightforward, and I'll guide you through it step-by-step.

1. Install Elixir

Elixir is the programming language we'll be using, and it needs to be installed on your system. Here's how:

- **Visit the Official Website:** Go to the official Elixir language website (elixir-lang.org) and navigate to the installation instructions.
- **Choose Your Operating System:** Select the installation guide that matches your operating system (macOS, Windows, Linux).
- **Follow the Instructions:** The guide will provide detailed instructions and download links. Typically, this involves downloading an installer or using a package manager.

Installing Elixir will also install **Mix**, which is Elixir's built-in build tool and package manager. We'll use Mix to create new projects, manage dependencies, and run tasks.

2. Install Phoenix

Phoenix is the web framework we'll use to build our Elixir applications. It provides a structured foundation for handling web requests, routing, and rendering templates. Here's how to install it:

- **Use Mix:** Open your terminal or command prompt and run the following command:

Bash

```
mix archive.install hex phx_new
```

This command uses Mix to download and install the phx_new archive, which contains the necessary tools for creating new Phoenix projects.

3. Install Node.js

While we'll primarily be working with Elixir, we'll still need Node.js for certain frontend tools and libraries. Node.js is a JavaScript runtime environment that allows you to run JavaScript outside of a web browser.

- **Download the Installer:** Go to the official Node.js website (nodejs.org) and download the installer for your operating system.
- **Run the Installer:** Follow the on-screen instructions to install Node.js. This will also install **npm** (Node Package Manager), which is used to manage JavaScript packages.

4. Choose a Code Editor

A good code editor is essential for writing and editing code. Here are some popular choices for Elixir development:

- **Visual Studio Code:** A free and highly extensible editor with excellent Elixir support through extensions.
- **Sublime Text:** A fast and lightweight editor with a strong community and many plugins for Elixir.
- **Atom:** A customizable editor developed by GitHub with good Elixir support.

Choose an editor that you're comfortable with and explore its features. A good editor will provide syntax highlighting, code completion, and debugging tools to make your development experience more efficient.

5. (Optional) Install a Database

If you plan on working with a database, PostgreSQL is a popular choice for Elixir applications. It's a robust and reliable relational database that integrates well with Phoenix.

- **Download and Install:** Visit the official PostgreSQL website (postgresql.org) and download the installer for your operating system. Follow the instructions to install it.

Verifying Your Installation

Once you've installed these tools, you can verify that everything is working correctly by opening your terminal and running the following commands:

- **Check Elixir Version:** elixir -v
- **Check Phoenix Version:** mix phx.new --version
- **Check Node.js Version:** node -v
- **Check npm Version:** npm -v

These commands should display the version numbers of the respective tools, indicating that they are installed correctly.

With your development environment set up, you're ready to start writing Elixir code and building exciting frontend applications. In the next chapter, we'll explore the fundamentals of HTML and CSS, which are essential for creating the structure and style of your web pages.

Chapter 2: HTML and CSS Fundamentals

Now that your development environment is all set up, let's get our hands dirty with the core technologies of the web: HTML and CSS. These two languages are the foundation of any web page, providing structure and style. Think of HTML as the architect that designs the blueprint of a house, and CSS as the interior designer that makes it look beautiful and functional.

2.1 Building Blocks of the Web: HTML

Alright, let's get up close and personal with HTML! As we mentioned earlier, HTML is like the architect of a web page. It provides the structure and defines the different elements that make up the content. Think of it as the blueprint that tells the browser how to display the information.

Tags: The Language of HTML

HTML uses a system of **tags** to mark up the content. Tags are keywords enclosed in angle brackets, like <p> for paragraph or <h1> for a level 1 heading. Most tags come in pairs: an opening tag (e.g., <p>) and a closing tag (e.g., </p>). The content you want to display goes between these tags.

Here's a simple example:

HTML

<p>This is a paragraph of text.</p>

This tells the browser to display "This is a paragraph of text." as a paragraph.

Elements: The Building Blocks

An HTML **element** consists of the opening tag, the content, and the closing tag. It represents a distinct component of the page, like a heading, a paragraph, an image, or a link.

Here are some of the most common HTML elements you'll encounter:

- **Headings:** <h1> to <h6> are used for headings, with <h1> being the most important and <h6> the least.
- **Paragraphs:** <p> defines a paragraph of text.
- **Links:** <a> creates hyperlinks to other pages or resources. It uses the **href** attribute to specify the URL. For example:

HTML

```
<a href="https://www.example.com">Visit Example.com</a>
```

- **Images:** <img> is used to embed images. The src attribute specifies the image file's location, and the alt attribute provides alternative text for accessibility. For example:

HTML

```
<img src="my-image.jpg" alt="A beautiful landscape">
```

- **Divisions:** <div> is a generic container for grouping other elements. It's often used for styling or layout purposes.
- **Spans:** <span> is used to style inline elements (within a block of text).

Attributes:

Attributes provide additional information about HTML elements. They are placed within the opening tag and consist of a name and a value, separated by an equals sign.

Here are some commonly used attributes:

- **src:** Specifies the source URL for an image or other embedded content.[9]
- **href:** Specifies the URL for a link.
- **class:** Assigns a class name to an element, which can be used for styling with CSS.
- **id:** Assigns a unique ID to an element, also useful for styling and scripting.
- **alt:** Provides alternative text for images, important for accessibility.[13]

Let's Get Practical: Building a Simple Web Page

Let's put these concepts into practice by creating a simple web page.

1. **Create an HTML file:** Open your code editor and create a new file named **index.html**.
2. **Add the basic structure:** Every HTML document needs a basic structure. Type the following code into your index.html file:

HTML

```
<!DOCTYPE html>

<html>

<head>

<title>My First Web Page</title>

</head>

<body>

</body>

</html>
```

- ○ **<!DOCTYPE html>**: Tells the browser it's an HTML5 document.
- ○ **<html>**: The root element of the page.
- ○ **<head>**: Contains meta-information about the page (like the title).
- ○ **<title>**: Sets the title that appears in the browser tab.
- ○ **<body>**: Contains the visible content of the page.
3. **Add some content:** Now, let's add some headings, paragraphs, and an image:

```
<!DOCTYPE html> <html> <head> <title>My First Web Page</title> </head> <body> <h1>Welcome to my website!</h1> <p>This is a paragraph of text.</p> <img src="my-image.jpg"[14] alt="A beautiful image"> </body> </html>
```

4. **Save and open in browser**: Save the `index.html` file and open it in your web browser. You should see your newly created web page with a heading, a paragraph, and an image (make sure you have an image named `my-image.jpg` in the same directory as your HTML file).

You've just created your first web page using HTML. It might not look fancy yet, but we'll add some style with CSS in the next section.

2.2 Styling with CSS

We've built the structure of our web page with HTML. Now it's time to make it look good with CSS! Think of CSS as your artistic toolkit for the web. It lets you add colors, change fonts, adjust spacing, and create beautiful layouts.

CSS Syntax:

CSS uses a set of rules to style HTML elements. Each rule consists of a **selector** and a **declaration block**.

- **Selector:** This specifies which HTML element(s) you want to style. It can be an element name, a class, an ID, or a combination of these.
- **Declaration Block:** This contains one or more declarations, each consisting of a **property** and a **value**, separated by a colon.

Here's the basic syntax:

CSS

```
selector {

property1: value1;

property2: value2;

/* ... more declarations ... */

}
```

Let's break down an example:

CSS

```
p {

color: blue;

font-size: 16px;

}
```

In this rule:

- p is the selector, targeting all paragraph elements (<p>).
- The declaration block contains two declarations:
  - **color: blue;** sets the text color to blue.
  - **font-size: 16px;** sets the font size to 16 pixels.

Types of Selectors: Targeting Elements

CSS provides a variety of selectors to target specific elements or groups of elements:

- **Element Selector:** Targets elements based on their tag name (e.g., **h1, p, div**).

- **Class Selector:** Targets elements with a specific class attribute. You define a class in HTML using the **class** attribute (e.g., **<p class="highlight">**). In CSS, you use a period (.) followed by the class name (e.g., .highlight { color: red; }).
- **ID Selector:** Targets a single element with a specific ID attribute. You define an ID in HTML using the **id** attribute (e.g., **<p id="intro">**). In CSS, you use a hash symbol (#) followed by the ID name (e.g., #intro { font-weight: bold; }).

Adding CSS to Your HTML

There are three main ways to add CSS to your HTML:

1. **Inline Styles:** You can add CSS directly to an HTML element using the **style** attribute. This is generally not recommended for larger projects, but it can be useful for quick styling.

HTML

```
<p style="color: green;">This paragraph has inline styles.</p>
```

2. **Internal Stylesheet:** You can include CSS within the <head> section of your HTML document using the <style> tag.

HTML

```
<!DOCTYPE html>

<html>
```

```html
<head>

<title>My Styled Page</title>

<style>

p {

color: purple;

}

</style>

</head>

<body>

<p>This paragraph is styled with an internal stylesheet.</p>

</body>

</html>
```

3. **External Stylesheet:** This is the most common and recommended method. You create a separate CSS file (e.g., **styles.css**) and link it to your HTML using the **<link>** tag in the **<head>** section.

HTML

```html
<!DOCTYPE html>

<html>
```

```
<head>
```

```
<title>My Styled Page</title>
```

```
<link rel="stylesheet" href="styles.css">
```

```
</head>
```

```
<body>
```

```
<p>This paragraph is styled with an external stylesheet.</p>
```

```
</body>
```

```
</html>
```

In your styles.css file, you would have:

CSS

```
p {
```

```
color: orange;
```

```
}
```

Let's Get Practical:

Let's add some style to the web page we created in the previous section.

1. **Create a CSS file:** In the same directory as your index.html file, create a new file named **styles.css**.
2. **Add some styles:** Open **styles.css** and add the following CSS code:

CSS

```css
body {

font-family: sans-serif;

margin: 20px;

}

h1 {

color: #333; /* Dark gray color */

text-align: center;

}

img {

display: block;

margin: 0 auto; /* Center the image */

max-width: 500px;

}
```

3. **Link the CSS file:** In your index.html file, add the following line within the <head> section:

HTML

```html
<link rel="stylesheet" href="styles.css">
```

4. **Save and refresh:** Save both files and refresh your web page in the browser. You should see the styles applied to your content.

Now you've got a styled web page! This is just a taste of what you can do with CSS. We'll explore more advanced styling techniques in the following sections.

2.3 Responsive Design

So you've built a beautiful web page with HTML and CSS. But here's the thing: people will be viewing your website on a whole bunch of different devices, from massive desktop screens to tiny smartphone screens. That's where responsive design comes in!

Responsive design is all about making sure your website looks good and functions well on any device, no matter the screen size or orientation. It's like having a magical website that can shapeshift to fit perfectly on any screen.

Why is Responsive Design Important?

- **User Experience:** A responsive website provides a better user experience. Visitors can easily read the content, navigate the site, and interact with elements without zooming or scrolling excessively.
- **Accessibility:** Responsive design makes your website accessible to a wider audience, including people with disabilities who might be using assistive technologies.

- **SEO Benefits:** Search engines favor websites that are mobile-friendly. A responsive design can improve your website's ranking in search results.

Media Queries:

The core technique for achieving responsive design is using **media queries**. Media queries allow you to apply different CSS styles based on characteristics of the device, such as:

- **Screen width:** You can target specific screen size ranges (e.g., styles for screens smaller than 768px).
- **Screen orientation:** You can apply different styles for portrait and landscape orientations.
- **Resolution:** You can target high-resolution screens for sharper images.

How Media Queries Work

Media queries use the @media rule followed by a condition and a set of CSS rules. Here's the basic syntax:

CSS

```css
@media (condition) {

/* CSS rules to apply when the condition is met */

}
```

Here's an example that applies styles for screens with a maximum width of 768 pixels:

CSS

```css
@media (max-width: 768px) {
```

```css
body {

font-size: 14px;

}

.container {

width: 90%;

}

}
```

In this example, when the screen width is 768px or smaller, the font size will be reduced to 14px, and the .container element will take up 90% of the screen width.

Let's Get Practical: Making Our Website Responsive

Let's make the web page we created earlier responsive.

1. **Target smaller screens**: Open your styles.css file and add the following media query:

CSS

```css
@media (max-width: 768px) {

body {

margin: 10px; /* Reduce margin on smaller screens */

}

h1 {
```

```
font-size: 24px; /* Reduce heading size */

}

img {

max-width: 100%; /* Make image responsive */

}

}
```

2. **Test it out:** Save your **styles.css** file and resize your browser window. You should see the styles change when the screen width goes below 768px. You can also test it on different devices (if you have access to them) to see how it looks.

Mobile-First Approach

A common approach in responsive design is the "mobile-first" strategy. This means you start by designing and styling for the smallest screen size first, and then progressively add styles for larger screens using media queries. This helps ensure a good experience on mobile devices and avoids unnecessary CSS overrides.

Beyond the Basics

There's much more to explore in responsive design, including:

- **Fluid Grids:** Using percentages for widths instead of fixed pixels.

- **Flexible Images:** Making images scale proportionally with the container.
- **Viewport Meta Tag:** Controlling how the page is scaled on different devices.

With practice and experimentation, you can master the art of responsive design and create websites that look fantastic on any device.

2.4 Accessibility Considerations

We've got a website that looks good and adapts to different screen sizes. Awesome! But there's one more crucial aspect we need to consider: accessibility.

Accessibility means making your website usable for everyone, including people with disabilities. This might include people with visual impairments, auditory impairments, motor impairments, or cognitive differences. It's about creating a web that's inclusive and allows everyone to access information and interact with your content.

Why is Accessibility Important?

- **It's the right thing to do:** Everyone deserves equal access to information and services on the web.
- **It reaches a wider audience:** People with disabilities represent a significant portion of the population.
- **It improves usability for everyone:** Many accessibility features benefit all users, not just those with disabilities.

- **It's often a legal requirement:** In many countries, there are laws and regulations requiring websites to be accessible.

Key Accessibility Principles

Here are some essential principles to keep in mind when designing and developing accessible websites:

1. Semantic HTML: Provide Meaning and Structure

Use semantic HTML elements to provide meaning and structure to your content. This means using elements like <article>, <nav>, <aside>, and <footer> for their intended purpose. This helps assistive technologies (like screen readers) understand the content and present it in a meaningful way to users.

2. Alternative Text for Images: Describe the Visuals

Always provide alternative text (**alt** text) for images using the **alt** attribute. This text describes the image to users who cannot see it. For example:

HTML

```
<img src="my-image.jpg" alt="A scenic mountain landscape with a clear blue sky">
```

If an image is purely decorative, you can use an empty alt attribute:

HTML

```
<img src="decorative-image.png" alt="">
```

3. Keyboard Navigation:

Ensure that all interactive elements (links, buttons, forms) can be accessed and used with a keyboard alone. This is important for people who cannot use a mouse or have limited motor control. You can test this by tabbing through your website using the Tab key and interacting with elements using the Enter or Space keys.

4. Color Contrast: Make it Readable

Use sufficient color contrast between text and background to make it readable for people with low vision. There are tools available online (like WebAIM's Color Contrast Checker) to help you check the contrast ratios of your colors.

5. ARIA Attributes: Provide Extra Information

ARIA (Accessible Rich Internet Applications) attributes provide additional information to assistive technologies about the[1] roles, states, and properties of elements. For example, you can use ARIA attributes to:

- Define the role of an element (e.g., role="button").
- Indicate whether an element is expanded or collapsed (e.g., aria-expanded="true").
- Associate labels with form fields (e.g., aria-labelledby="label-id").

Let's Get Practical:

Let's revisit our example web page and make some accessibility improvements.

1. **Add alt text to the image:** Make sure your <img> tag has an appropriate alt attribute:

HTML

```
<img src="my-image.jpg" alt="A beautiful image for my website">
```

2. **Check color contrast:** Use a color contrast checker tool to ensure that the text color and background color have sufficient contrast. If not, adjust the colors accordingly.
3. **Use semantic HTML (if applicable):** If your content has sections that could benefit from semantic elements (like <article>, <nav>, or <aside>), add those elements to your HTML structure.

Testing Accessibility

There are various tools and techniques for testing the accessibility of your website:

- **Automated Tools:** Tools like WAVE and Lighthouse can identify many accessibility issues automatically.
- **Manual Testing:** Manually test your website using a keyboard, screen reader, and other assistive technologies.
- **User Testing:** Conduct user testing with people with disabilities to get real-world feedback.

By incorporating accessibility considerations into your web development process, you can create websites that are inclusive and usable for everyone.

Chapter 3: Introduction to JavaScript

While this book champions Elixir and LiveView for frontend development, having a grasp of JavaScript fundamentals is invaluable. Think of it like this: even though you might have a fantastic chef cooking your meals (that's Elixir and LiveView!), it's still handy to know some basic kitchen skills! JavaScript is that essential knowledge in the web development kitchen. It's the language that brings interactivity to websites, allowing you to create dynamic and engaging user experiences.

3.1 JavaScript Basics

Let's get acquainted with the basics of JavaScript! Think of JavaScript as the language that brings your web pages to life. It adds interactivity, dynamic updates, and all sorts of cool features to make your website more engaging.

Variables:

In JavaScript, **variables** are like containers that hold information. You can give them names and store different types of data in them, like numbers, text, or even true/false values.

To create a variable, you use the var, let, or const keyword, followed by the name you want to give it.

JavaScript

```
var myName = "Alice";

let age = 30;

const PI = 3.14159;
```

- **var** is the older way to declare variables.
- **let** is used for variables that might change their value later.
- **const** is used for variables that should remain constant (their value cannot be reassigned).

Data Types:

JavaScript has several data types to represent different kinds of information:

- **Strings:** Text enclosed in single or double quotes (e.g., "Hello", 'World').
- **Numbers:** Numeric values (e.g., 10, 3.14, -5).
- **Booleans:** Represent **true** or **false** values.
- **Objects:** Collections of key-value pairs (like a dictionary).
- **Arrays:** Ordered lists of values (e.g., [1, 2, 3]).
- **Null:** Represents the intentional absence of a value.
- **Undefined:** Represents a variable that has been declared but has not been assigned a value.

Operators: Performing Actions

Operators are symbols that perform actions on data. Here are some common types:

- **Arithmetic Operators:** +, -, *, /, % (modulo - gives the remainder of a division).

JavaScript

```
let sum = 5 + 3; // sum will be 8
```

```
let product = 4 * 7; // product will be 28
```

- **Assignment Operators:** =, +=, -=, *=, /=.

JavaScript

```
let x = 10;
```

```
x += 5; // x will now be 15 (same as x = x + 5)
```

- **Comparison Operators:** == (loosely equal to), === (strictly equal to), != (not equal to), > (greater than), < (less than), >= (greater than or equal to), <= (less than or equal to).

JavaScript

```
let a = 5;
```

```
let b = "5";
```

```
console.log(a == b);  // true (loose comparison, converts types)
```

```
console.log(a === b); // false (strict comparison, checks types)
```

- **Logical Operators:** && (and), || (or), ! (not).

JavaScript

```javascript
let isAdult = age >= 18;

let hasLicense = true;

let canDrive = isAdult && hasLicense; // canDrive will be
true if both conditions are true
```

Control Flow:

Control flow statements determine the order in which your code is executed.

- **Conditional Statements:** if, else if, else allow you to execute different blocks of code based on conditions.

JavaScript

```javascript
let temperature = 25;

if (temperature > 30) {

console.log("It's a hot day!");

} else if (temperature > 20) {

console.log("It's a pleasant day.");

} else {

console.log("It's¹ a bit cool.");

}
```

- **Loops:** for and while loops allow you to repeat blocks of code.

JavaScript

```javascript
// Print numbers from 1 to 5

for (let i = 1; i <= 5; i++) {

console.log(i);

}

let count = 0;

while (count < 3) {

console.log("Count:", count);

count++;

}
```

Functions:

Functions are like mini-programs within your code. They allow you to group a set of statements together and give them a name. You can then "call" the function by its name to execute those statements whenever you need them.

JavaScript

```javascript
function greet(name) {

console.log("Hello, " + name + "!");
```

```
}
```

greet("Bob"); // Outputs "Hello, Bob!"

greet("Alice"); // Outputs "Hello, Alice!"

Let's Get Practical:

1. **Create an HTML file:** Create a new file called index.html.
2. **Add a script tag:** Inside the <body> of your HTML, add a <script> tag.

HTML

```html
<!DOCTYPE html>

<html>

<head>

<title>JavaScript Basics</title>

</head>

<body>

<script>

// Your JavaScript code will go here

</script>

</body>

</html>
```

3. **Write some JavaScript:** Inside the <script> tag, add the following code:

JavaScript

```
let name = prompt("What's your name?");

alert("Hello, " + name + "!");
```

4. **Save and open in browser:** Save the **index.html** file and open it in your web browser. You'll be prompted to enter your name, and then an alert box will greet you.

This simple example demonstrates how JavaScript can interact with the user by taking input and displaying output. You've now got a taste of the power of JavaScript!

3.2 DOM Manipulation

Now that you have a handle on JavaScript basics, let's explore how to interact with the structure of your web page using the **Document Object Model (DOM)**. Think of the DOM as a bridge between your JavaScript code and the HTML content. It allows you to select elements, modify their content, change their styles, and even add or remove elements dynamically.

The DOM:

When your web browser loads an HTML document, it creates a tree-like representation of the page's structure. This representation is called the DOM. Each HTML element becomes a **node** in this tree, and you can use JavaScript to navigate and manipulate these nodes.

Selecting Elements:

Before you can do anything with an element, you need to select it. JavaScript provides several methods for selecting elements:

- **getElementById():** This method selects an element based on its unique id attribute.

JavaScript

```
const myHeading = document.getElementById("myHeading");
```

- **getElementsByClassName():** This method selects all elements with a specific class attribute. It returns a collection of elements (an HTMLCollection).

JavaScript

```
const paragraphs = document.getElementsByClassName("paragraph");
```

- **getElementsByTagName():** This method selects all elements with a given tag name. It also returns an HTMLCollection.

JavaScript

```
const links = document.getElementsByTagName("a");
```

- **querySelector()**: This method selects the *first* element that matches a given CSS selector.

JavaScript

```
const firstLink = document.querySelector("a");
```

- **querySelectorAll()**: This method selects *all* elements that match a given CSS selector. It returns a NodeList.

JavaScript

```
const allLinks = document.querySelectorAll("a");
```

Modifying Content:

Once you've selected an element, you can modify its content in various ways:

- **textContent**: This property gets or sets the text content of an element.

JavaScript

```
myHeading.textContent = "New Heading Text!";
```

- innerHTML: This property gets or sets the HTML content of an element.

JavaScript

```
myParagraph.innerHTML    =    "<p>This    is
<strong>new</strong> content!</p>";
```

- setAttribute(): This method sets the value of an attribute for an element.

JavaScript

myImage.setAttribute("src", "new-image.jpg");

Styling Elements:

You can also use JavaScript to modify the style of elements. You access an element's style properties through its style object.

JavaScript

myHeading.style.color = "blue";

myHeading.style.fontSize = "30px";

Let's Get Practical:

1. **Create an HTML file:** Create a new file called dom-example.html.
2. **Add some HTML content:** Add the following HTML code to your file:

HTML

```
<!DOCTYPE html>

<html>

<head>

<title>DOM Manipulation</title>
```

```
</head>

<body>

<h1 id="myHeading">Hello!</h1>

<p class="paragraph">This is a paragraph.</p>

<button id="myButton">Click Me</button>

<script>

// Your JavaScript code will go here

</script>

</body>

</html>
```

3. **Add JavaScript:** Inside the <script> tag, add the following JavaScript code:

JavaScript

```
// Select elements

const heading = document.getElementById("myHeading");

const button = document.getElementById("myButton");

// Change heading text when the button is clicked

button.addEventListener("click", function() {

heading.textContent = "Button Clicked!";
```

```
heading.style.color = "green";

});
```

4. **Save and open in browser:** Save the **dom-example.html** file and open it in your web browser. You should see a heading, a paragraph, and a button. When you click the button, the heading text and color will change.

This example demonstrates how to select elements, modify their content and style, and handle events using JavaScript and the DOM. You're now well on your way to creating dynamic and interactive web experiences!

3.3 Working with APIs

Let's step into the world of APIs! API stands for **Application Programming Interface**. Think of an API as a waiter in a restaurant. You (your web page) are the customer, and the kitchen (another application or server) has all the delicious data you want. The API takes your order (your request), goes to the kitchen, gets the data you requested, and brings it back to you.

APIs allow different applications to communicate and exchange data with each other. This lets you fetch information from external sources and integrate it into your web page. For example, you could use an API to display weather information, get the latest news headlines, or show tweets from a specific user.

Making API Requests: How to Order Your Data

The **fetch()** API is a powerful tool in JavaScript for making requests to APIs. Here's the basic syntax:

JavaScript

```
fetch(url)

.then(response => response.json())

.then(data => {

// Process the data

})

.catch(error => {

// Handle errors

});
```

Let's break it down:

1. **fetch(url)**: This initiates a request to the API endpoint specified by the **url**.
2. **.then(response => response.json())**: This part handles the response from the API.
   - **response.json()** parses the response as JSON (JavaScript Object Notation), a common data format for APIs.
3. **.then(data => { ... })**: This part receives the parsed JSON data and allows you to do something with it, like display it on your web page.

4. **.catch(error => { ... })**: This part handles any errors that occur during the request.

JSON: The Language of APIs

JSON (JavaScript Object Notation) is a lightweight data format that's commonly used for exchanging data between web servers and clients. It's easy for humans to read and write and easy for machines to parse and generate. JSON data is represented as key-value pairs, similar to JavaScript[1] objects.

Let's Get Practical: Fetching Data from an API

Let's build a simple example that fetches data from a public API and displays it on a web page. We'll use the JSONPlaceholder API (https://jsonplaceholder.typicode.com/), which provides fake data for testing purposes.

1. **Create an HTML file:** Create a new file called api-example.html.
2. **Add HTML structure:** Add the following HTML to your file:

HTML

<!DOCTYPE html>

<html>

<head>

<title>API Example</title>

```html
</head>

<body>

<h1>Posts</h1>

<ul id="posts-list"></ul>

<script>

// Your JavaScript code will go here

</script>

</body>

</html>
```

3. **Add JavaScript:** Inside the <script> tag, add the following JavaScript code:

JavaScript

```javascript
const postsList = document.getElementById("posts-list");

fetch('https://jsonplaceholder.typicode.com/posts')

.then(response => response.json()) .then(posts² => { posts.forEach(post => { const listItem = document.createElement("li"); listItem.textContent = post.title; postsList.appendChild(listItem);³ }); }) .catch(error => { console.error('Error fetching posts:', error); }); ```
```

4. **Save and open in browser:** Save the api-example.html file and open it in your browser. You should see a list of post titles fetched from the JSONPlaceholder API.

This example demonstrates how to use **fetch()** to make an API request, parse the JSON response, and dynamically update the web page with the retrieved data. You've now unlocked the ability to bring external data into your web applications!

3.4 Modern JavaScript (ES6+)

Alright, let's step into the future of JavaScript! In 2015, JavaScript went through a major upgrade with the release of ECMAScript 2015 (also known as ES6). This update brought a whole bunch of cool new features that make JavaScript more powerful, expressive, and enjoyable to write.

Arrow Functions:

Arrow functions provide a more concise syntax for writing functions. They are especially handy for short, simple functions.

JavaScript

```
// Traditional function

function add(a, b) {

return a + b;

}
```

```
// Arrow function
```

```
const add = (a, b) => a + b;
```

Arrow functions are more compact. If the function body has only one expression, you can even omit the curly braces {} and the return keyword.

Template Literals: Easier String Formatting

Template literals make it easier to work with strings, especially when you need to embed variables or expressions within them. They use backticks (``) instead of single or double quotes.

JavaScript

```
const name = "Alice";
```

```
const age = 30;
```

```
// Traditional string concatenation
```

```
console.log("Hello, " + name + "! You are " + age + " years old.");
```

```
// Template literal
```

```
console.log(`Hello, ${name}! You are ${age} years old.`);
```

Template literals make your code more readable and avoid the awkward plus signs (+) for concatenation.

Destructuring:

Destructuring allows you to easily extract values from objects and arrays.

JavaScript

```
const person = { name: "Bob", age: 30, city: "New York" };

// Traditional way to access properties

const name = person.name;

const age = person.age;

// Destructuring

const { name, age } = person;
```

Destructuring makes your code cleaner and avoids repetitive code for accessing object properties or array elements.

Modules: Organizing Your Code

Modules help you organize your JavaScript code into separate files, making it easier to manage and maintain larger projects.

- **export:** Use the **export** keyword to make variables, functions, or classes available from a module.

JavaScript

```
// in myModule.js

export function greet(name) {
```

```
console.log(`Hello, ${name}!`);
```

}

- **import**: Use the **import** keyword to bring in exported members from a module.

JavaScript

```
// in main.js

import { greet } from './myModule.js';

greet("Alice");
```

Let's Get Practical: Using ES6+ Features

Let's create a simple example that uses some of these ES6+ features.

1. **Create two files:** Create two files named **main.js** and **utils.js**.
2. **Write a module:** In **utils.js**, add the following code:

JavaScript

```
export const PI = 3.14159;

export function calculateArea(radius) {

return PI * radius * radius;

}
```

3. **Import and use the module:** In main.js, add the following code:

JavaScript

```javascript
import { PI, calculateArea } from './utils.js';


const radius = 5;

const area = calculateArea(radius);

console.log(`The area of a circle with radius ${radius} is ${area}`)
```

4. **Create an HTML file:** Create an index.html file and include **main.js** using a <script> tag with the **type="module"** attribute.

HTML

```html
<!DOCTYPE html>

<html>

<head>

<title>ES6+ Features</title>

</head>

<body>

<script type="module" src="main.js"></script>
```

```
</body>

</html>
```

5. **Open in browser:** Open index.html in your browser, and you should see the calculated area logged in the console.

This example demonstrates how to use modules, arrow functions, and template literals. These are just a few of the many powerful features introduced in ES6+. By embracing modern JavaScript, you can write cleaner, more efficient, and more maintainable code.

Chapter 4: Phoenix Framework Fundamentals

It's time to dive into the heart of Elixir web development: the Phoenix framework! Phoenix is a powerful and productive web framework written in Elixir. It provides a solid foundation for building scalable, fault-tolerant, and maintainable web applications. Think of it as your trusty toolkit for constructing amazing web experiences with Elixir.

4.1 MVC Architecture in Phoenix

Let's break down how Phoenix organizes your code using the **Model-View-Controller (MVC)** architecture. Think of MVC as a way to keep things tidy and efficient in your web application. It's like having separate compartments in your toolbox for different types of tools – you know where everything is, and it's easier to find the right tool for the job.

The MVC Trio:

In the MVC pattern, your application's code is divided into three interconnected parts:

- **Models:** These are the brainy part of your application. They represent the data and the rules for how that data should behave. In Phoenix, models are often defined using Ecto schemas, which we'll explore in more detail later. For now, just think of them as blueprints for your data.

- **Views:** Views are the artists. They take the data from the models and transform it into a presentable format, usually HTML, that the user can see in their browser. Phoenix uses templates written in EEx (Elixir's templating language) to create these views.
- **Controllers:** These are the managers. They act as intermediaries between the models and the views. They handle incoming web requests, talk to the models to get or update data, and then pass that data to the views for rendering.

Why MVC? Benefits of Separation

The beauty of MVC lies in its separation of concerns. Each component has a specific role, making your code:

- **Modular:** You can work on different parts of your application independently.
- **Maintainable:** It's easier to understand, debug, and update your code when it's well-organized.
- **Testable:** You can test each component (models, views, controllers) in isolation.
- **Reusable:** You can reuse components in different parts of your application.

Let's Get Practical:

Let's create a simple Phoenix application to see MVC in action.

1. **Create a new Phoenix project:** Open your terminal and run the following command:

Bash

```
mix phx.new my_mvc_app
cd my_mvc_app
```

2. **Create a controller:** Generate a controller named GreetingController with an action called hello:

Bash

```
mix phx.gen.html Greeting greeting hello
```

3. **Define the action:** Open the generated controller file (**lib/my_mvc_app_web/controllers/greeting_contr oller.ex**) and modify the **hello** action:

Elixir

```
defmodule MyMvcAppWeb.GreetingController do
use MyMvcAppWeb, :controller
def hello(conn, _params) do
name = "World" # This is our "model" data for now
render(conn, "hello.html", name: name)
end
end
```

4. **Update the view:** Open the generated view template file (**lib/my_mvc_app_web/templates/greeting/hello.h tml.eex**) and update it:

HTML

```
<h1>Hello, <%= @name %>!</h1>
```

5. **Define the route:** Open the router file (lib/my_mvc_app_web/router.ex) and add a route for the hello action:

Elixir

```
scope "/", MyMvcAppWeb do
pipe_through :browser
get "/hello", GreetingController, :hello
end
```

6. **Start the server:** Run **mix phx.server** to start the Phoenix server.
7. **Visit the page:** Open your browser and go to **http://localhost:4000/hello**. You should see "Hello, World!" displayed on the page.

Explanation:

- **Model:** In this simple example, the **name** variable in the controller acts as our model data.
- **View:** The **hello.html.eex** template renders the greeting message using the @name variable passed from the controller.
- **Controller:** The hello action in GreetingController sets the **name** variable and renders the view.
- **Route:** The route /hello maps to the hello action in **GreetingController**.

This example demonstrates the basic flow of data in an MVC application. As you build more complex applications, you'll see how this pattern helps you organize and manage your code effectively.

4.2 Routing and Request Handling

Let's explore how Phoenix handles incoming web requests and directs them to the appropriate parts of your application. Think of routing as a traffic controller for your website, ensuring that each request reaches its correct destination.

The Router: Your Website's Traffic Controller

Phoenix uses a router file (**router.ex**) to define the routes for your application. This file acts like a map, telling Phoenix which controller action should handle a specific incoming request.

Defining Routes: Mapping Requests to Actions

Routes are defined using macros like **get**, **post**, **put**, and **delete**, which correspond to HTTP verbs (GET, POST, PUT, DELETE). These verbs indicate the type of action the client wants to perform:

- **get**: Retrieve data (e.g., viewing a page).
- **post**: Create new data (e.g., submitting a form).
- **put**: Update existing data.
- **delete**: Delete data.

Here's a simple example:

Elixir

```
# lib/my_app_web/router.ex
scope "/", MyAppWeb do
pipe_through :browser
get "/", PageController, :index
post "/submit", FormController, :submit
end
```

In this example:

- A **GET** request to / (the root URL) will be handled by the **index** action in **PageController**.
- A **POST** request to /**submit** (e.g., submitting a form) will be handled by the **submit** action in **FormController**.

Route Helpers:

Phoenix provides helper functions to generate URLs for your routes. This makes it easier to create links within your application without hardcoding URLs.

For example, if you have a route defined as **get "/users/:id"**, **UserController**, :show, you can generate the URL for a specific user with:

Elixir

```
<%= link "View User", to: Routes.user_path(@conn, :show, user.id) %>
```

Pipelines:

Pipelines are a way to group a series of plugs (modular functions) that process requests before they reach your controllers. Phoenix provides some built-in pipelines, such as :**browser**, which handles things like fetching session data and serving static assets.

Let's Get Practical:

Let's create a Phoenix application with a couple of routes to see how routing works.

1. **Create a new Phoenix project:** If you haven't already, create a new project:

Bash

```
mix phx.new my_routing_app
cd my_routing_app
```

2. **Create a controller:** Generate a controller named **PageController** with an action called **about**:

Bash

```
mix phx.gen.html Page page about
```

3. **Define the action:** Open the generated controller file (**lib/my_routing_app_web/controllers/page_controller.ex**) and add an **about** action:

Elixir

```
defmodule MyRoutingAppWeb.PageController do
use MyRoutingAppWeb, :controller
def index(conn, _params) do
```

```elixir
render(conn, "index.html")
end
def about(conn, _params) do
render(conn, "about.html")
end
end
```

4. **Define the routes:** Open the router file (lib/my_routing_app_web/router.ex) and add a route for the about action:

Elixir

```elixir
scope "/", MyRoutingAppWeb do
pipe_through :browser
get "/", PageController, :index
get "/about", PageController, :about
end
```

5. **Start the server:** Run **mix phx.server** to start the server.
6. **Visit the pages:**
   ○ Open your browser and go to **http://localhost:4000/**. You should see the default Phoenix welcome page.
   ○ Go to **http://localhost:4000/about**. You should see the "About" page.

This example demonstrates how to define simple routes and handle requests with controllers. As your application grows, you can define more complex routes with dynamic segments and nested scopes to organize your URLs effectively.

4.3 Working with Ecto

Alright, it's time to talk about data! Almost every web application needs to interact with a database to store and retrieve information.[1] In Phoenix, we use Ecto to make this process smooth and enjoyable.[2] Think of Ecto as a friendly translator between your Elixir code and your database.

What is Ecto?

Ecto is a powerful database wrapper and query language for Elixir.[3] It provides a set of tools and abstractions that make it easier to work with databases like PostgreSQL, MySQL, and SQLite.[4] Ecto helps you:

- **Define schemas:** Schemas describe the structure of your data (like tables in a database).[5]
- **Write queries:** Ecto provides a way to write database queries in Elixir syntax.[6]
- **Handle changesets:** Changesets help you track and validate changes to your data before saving it to the database.[7]
- **Manage database connections:** Ecto takes care of connecting to the database and managing transactions.[8]

Schemas: Blueprints for Your Data

Schemas define the structure of your database tables and how they map to Elixir structs.[9] They're like blueprints that tell Ecto what kind of data you'll be storing.

Elixir

```elixir
# lib/my_app/blog/post.ex
defmodule MyApp.Blog.Post do
use Ecto.Schema
import Ecto.Changeset
schema "posts" do
field :title, :string
field :body, :text
field :published, :boolean, default: false
timestamps()
end
@doc false
def changeset(post, attrs) do
post
|> cast(attrs, [:title, :body, :published])
|> validate_required([:title, :body])
end
end
```

In this example, we define a schema for a **Post** with fields for **title**, **body**, and **published**. The **timestamps()** macro adds **inserted_at** and **updated_at** fields automatically.

Changesets:

Changesets are a powerful mechanism in Ecto for tracking and validating changes to your data.[10] They help ensure that only valid data is saved to the database.

In the **changeset** function above, we:

- **Cast** the incoming data (**attrs**) to the allowed fields ([:title, :body, :published]).
- **Validate** that the **title** and **body** fields are present.

You can add more validations, like checking data types, lengths, or uniqueness.[11]

Repositories:

Repositories provide functions for interacting with the database, such as inserting, updating, and retrieving data.[12]

Elixir

```
# lib/my_app/blog/post_repository.ex
defmodule MyApp.Blog.PostRepository do
use Ecto.Repo,
otp_app: :my_app,
adapter: Ecto.Adapters.Postgres
end
```

Let's Get Practical:

Let's create a simple blog application to see Ecto in action.

1. **Create a new Phoenix project:** If you haven't already, create a new project:

Bash

```
mix phx.new my_blog
cd my_blog
```

2. **Create a Post context:** Generate a context module for managing posts:

Bash

```
mix phx.gen.html Blog Post posts title:string body:text published:boolean
mix phx.gen.context Blog Post posts title:string body:text published:boolean
```

3. **Start the server:** Run `mix phx.server` to start the server.
4. **Use the generated CRUD interface:** Phoenix generates a basic CRUD (Create, Read, Update, Delete) interface for managing posts. You can access it in your browser at http://localhost:4000/posts.

Explanation:

- The `mix phx.gen.html` and `mix phx.gen.context` commands generate the necessary files for managing posts (schema, controller, views, templates, and repository).
- The generated code provides basic functionality for creating, viewing, editing, and deleting blog posts.

This example demonstrates how to use Ecto to define schemas, create changesets, and interact with the database. As you build more complex applications, you'll learn how to write custom queries, handle associations between different schemas, and perform more advanced database operations.

4.4 Authentication and Authorization

Now that we have a handle on data management with Ecto, let's talk about security! Authentication and authorization are crucial aspects of many web applications. They help you control who can access your app and what they're allowed to do.

Authentication:

Authentication is the process of verifying a user's identity. It's like showing your ID card to enter a building. In web applications, this usually involves:

- **User accounts:** Users create accounts with usernames (or emails) and passwords.
- **Login:** Users provide their credentials to log in.
- **Verification:** The application verifies the credentials against stored data (usually hashed passwords for security).
- **Session management:** Once authenticated, the application maintains a session to remember the user.

Authorization:

Authorization is the process of determining what a user is allowed to do after they've been authenticated. It's like having different levels of access within a building – some people might have access to all areas, while others might only have access to certain rooms.

Implementing Authentication in Phoenix

Phoenix offers several ways to implement authentication:

- **Rolling your own:** You can implement authentication from scratch, but this requires careful consideration of security best practices.
- **Phx.Gen.Auth:** This built-in generator provides a starting point for authentication with basic features.
- **Third-party libraries:** Libraries like Pow and Guardian offer more advanced and customizable authentication solutions.

Let's Get Practical:

Let's use **Phx.Gen.Auth** to add authentication to a Phoenix application.

1. **Create a new Phoenix project:** If you haven't already, create a new project:

Bash

```
mix phx.new my_auth_app
cd my_auth_app
```

2. **Install dependencies:** Fetch and install the necessary dependencies.

Bash

```
mix deps.get
```

3. **Generate authentication:** Run the phx.gen.auth generator:

Bash

mix phx.gen.auth Accounts User users
This will generate the necessary modules and files for user accounts and authentication.

4. **Migrate the database:** Run the migrations to create the users table:

Bash

mix ecto.migrate

5. **Start the server:** Run mix phx.server to start the server.
6. **Access authentication features:** You now have authentication features available:
   - **Registration:** Go to http://localhost:4000/users/register to create a new account.
   - **Login:** Go to http://localhost:4000/users/log_in to log in.
   - **Logout:** After logging in, you'll see a logout link.

Explanation:

- **Phx.Gen.Auth** generates a user schema, controllers, views, and templates for registration, login, and logout.
- It also provides basic security features like password hashing and session management.

Authorization with Plugs

Plugs are modular functions that can be used to process requests before they reach your controllers. You can use plugs to implement authorization rules.

Elixir

```elixir
defmodule MyAppWeb.Plugs.RequireAuth do
import Plug.Conn
import Phoenix.Controller
alias MyAppWeb.Router.Helpers, as: Routes
def init(opts), do: opts
def call(conn, _opts) do
if conn.assigns[:current_user] do
conn
else
conn
|> put_flash(:error, "You must¹ be logged in.")
|> redirect(to: Routes.user_session_path(conn, :new))
|> halt()
end
end
end
```

This plug checks if a current_user is assigned to the connection. If not, it redirects the user to the login page.

You can then use this plug in your controllers or router:

Elixir

```elixir
# In your controller
```

```
plug MyAppWeb.Plugs.RequireAuth when action in [:edit,
:update, :delete]
# Or in your router
pipeline :protected do
plug MyAppWeb.Plugs.RequireAuth
end
scope "/admin", MyAppWeb do
pipe_through [:browser, :protected]
# Protected routes here
end
```

This example demonstrates basic authentication and authorization with **Phx.Gen.Auth** and plugs. For more advanced scenarios, you might explore third-party libraries like Pow or Guardian, which offer more features and customization options.

Chapter 5: Introduction to LiveView

Get ready for the real magic to happen! It's time to explore LiveView, the game-changing feature of Phoenix that allows you to build dynamic, real-time user interfaces with the ease and elegance of Elixir. Think of LiveView as a superpower that lets you create interactive web experiences without writing tons of JavaScript.

5.1 The LiveView Philosophy

Let's delve into the core ideas behind LiveView! LiveView introduces a fresh perspective on building dynamic web interfaces. It challenges the conventional approach of relying heavily on client-side JavaScript and brings the power of Elixir to the forefront of frontend development.

The Traditional Approach:

Traditionally, building dynamic web pages involved a lot of JavaScript. You'd write JavaScript code to:

- Handle user interactions (clicks, form submissions, etc.).
- Send requests to the server to fetch or update data.
- Update the page content based on the server's response.

This often led to complex client-side logic and a lot of back-and-forth communication between the browser and the server.

The LiveView Approach: Server-Side Superpowers

LiveView flips the script by moving most of the heavy lifting to the server. Here's the gist:

1. **Server-Side Rendering:** The initial page is rendered on the server using Elixir and sent to the browser as HTML.
2. **Persistent Connection:** LiveView establishes a persistent connection between the browser and the server using WebSockets. This connection acts like a real-time communication channel.
3. **Server-Side Events:** When a user interacts with the page, the event is sent to the server over the WebSocket connection.
4. **State Management and Updates:** The server processes the event, updates the application's state, and re-renders the necessary parts of the HTML.
5. **Efficient Updates:** LiveView sends only the *changed* parts of the HTML back to the browser, which are then seamlessly patched into the existing page. This is called **DOM patching**, and it makes updates incredibly fast and efficient.

Why This Matters:

This server-centric approach offers several advantages:

- **Less JavaScript:** You can build rich, interactive interfaces with minimal or no JavaScript. This reduces complexity and makes your code easier to maintain.
- **Real-time Updates:** LiveView is perfect for applications that require real-time updates, such as

chat applications, collaborative tools, and live dashboards.

- **Improved Performance**: Server-side rendering and DOM patching can lead to faster initial page loads and smoother updates.
- **Simplified Development**: You can leverage Elixir's concurrency, fault-tolerance, and elegant syntax for both frontend and backend logic.

Let's Get Practical:

Let's create a basic LiveView to see this philosophy in action. We'll build a page that displays a random greeting every time it's refreshed.

1. **Create a new Phoenix project**: If you haven't already, create a new project:

Bash

```
mix phx.new my_liveview_app
cd my_liveview_app
```

2. **Create a LiveView**: Generate a LiveView module named GreetingLive:

Bash

```
mix phx.gen.live Greeting greeting
```

3. **Define the LiveView**: Open the generated LiveView file

(lib/my_liveview_app_web/live/greeting_live.ex) and update it:

Elixir

```elixir
defmodule MyLiveviewAppWeb.GreetingLive do
use MyLiveviewAppWeb, :live_view
def mount(_params, _session, socket) do
{:ok, assign(socket, greeting: get_random_greeting())}
end
def render(assigns) do
~L"""
<h1><%= @greeting %></h1>
"""
end
defp get_random_greeting do
["Hello!", "Hi there!", "Howdy!", "Greetings!"]
|> Enum.random()
end
end
```

4. **Define the route:** Open the router file (lib/my_liveview_app_web/router.ex) and add a route for GreetingLive:

Elixir

```elixir
scope "/", MyLiveviewAppWeb do
pipe_through :browser
live "/greeting", GreetingLive
end
```

5. **Start the server:** Run **mix phx.server** to start the server.

6. **Visit the page:** Open your browser and go to **http://localhost:4000/greeting**. You should see a random greeting. Refresh the page to see a different greeting.

Explanation:

- **mount:** This function is called when the LiveView is first mounted. It sets a random greeting using the get_random_greeting function.
- **render:** This function renders the HTML template, displaying the greeting.

Even in this simple example, you can see how LiveView handles the dynamic update of the greeting without any JavaScript. This is the core philosophy of LiveView — leverage the server's power to create dynamic and interactive web experiences.

5.2 Building Your First LiveView

Let's get our hands dirty and build a real LiveView! We'll create a simple counter application that lets you increment a number with the click of a button. This will give you a taste of how LiveView handles user interactions and updates the page dynamically.

Setting the Stage:

If you haven't already, let's create a fresh Phoenix project to house our LiveView masterpiece.

1. **Create a new project:** Open your terminal and run:

Bash

```
mix phx.new my_liveview_app
cd my_liveview_app
```

Generating the LiveView:

Phoenix provides a handy generator to create the basic structure of a LiveView.

2. **Generate the LiveView:** Run the following command in your terminal:

Bash

```
mix phx.gen.live Counter counter
```

3. This command creates a LiveView module named CounterLive and a corresponding template file.

The LiveView Code: Bringing it to Life

Now, let's open the generated LiveView file (**lib/my_liveview_app_web/live/counter_live.ex**) and add some code to make our counter functional.

3. **Update the LiveView module:** Replace the contents of **counter_live.ex** with the following:

Elixir

```elixir
defmodule MyLiveviewAppWeb.CounterLive do
use MyLiveviewAppWeb, :live_view
def mount(_params, _session, socket) do
{:ok, assign(socket, count: 0)}
end
def render(assigns) do
~L"""
<div>
Count: <%= @count %>
<button phx-click="increment">Increment</button>
</div>
"""
end
def handle_event("increment", _value, socket) do
{:noreply, update(socket, :count, &(&1 + 1))}
end
end
```

Wiring Up the Route:

We need to tell Phoenix how to access our LiveView. This is done in the router file.

4. **Update the router:** Open lib/my_liveview_app_web/router.ex and add the following route within the scope "/", MyLiveviewAppWeb block:

Elixir

```elixir
live "/counter", CounterLive
```

Starting the Server:

Now, let's fire up the Phoenix server and see our LiveView in action.

5. **Start the server:** Run **mix phx.server** in your terminal.
6. **Visit the page:** Open your browser and go to http://localhost:4000/counter.

You should see a page with a counter initialized to 0 and a button labeled "Increment". Click the button, and watch the magic happen – the counter increases in real-time without any page reloads!

Code Breakdown: Understanding the Pieces

Let's dissect the code to understand how it works:

- **mount function:** This function is called when the LiveView is first initialized. It sets the initial state of the **socket** (the connection between the browser and the server). Here, we use **assign** to assign a **count** of 0 to the socket.
- **render function:** This function is responsible for rendering the HTML that the user sees. It uses a special syntax called ~L to define a LiveView template. The <%= @count %> part dynamically displays the value of the **count** assigned to the socket.
- **phx-click attribute:** This attribute in the <button> tag tells LiveView to send an "increment" event to the server when the button is clicked.
- **handle_event function:** This function is called when the server receives the "increment" event. It uses the

update function to increment the **count** in the socket's state.

You've built your first LiveView. This simple example demonstrates the core principles of LiveView – handling events, updating state, and re-rendering the UI seamlessly. As you explore further, you'll discover how to build more complex and interactive applications with LiveView.

5.3 LiveView Lifecycle

let's take a closer look at how a LiveView functions over time. Understanding the LiveView lifecycle is like knowing the steps of a dance – it helps you predict what comes next and move gracefully with the rhythm of the application.

The Lifecycle Stages:

A LiveView goes through a series of stages, each with its own purpose:

1. **Mount:** This is the opening act, where the LiveView is first initialized. It's like setting up the stage and getting everything ready for the performance. The **mount** function is responsible for:
   - Establishing the initial state of the LiveView.
   - Assigning values to the socket (the connection between the browser and the server).
   - Potentially fetching initial data from the database.

2. **Handle Params:** This stage is like fine-tuning the performance based on the audience's requests. The handle_params function is called:
   - When the LiveView is first mounted.
   - When the URL parameters change (e.g., through live_patch or live_redirect).
   - It allows you to update the socket's state based on the URL parameters.
3. **Handle Event:** This is where the interaction happens! The handle_event function is the star of the show, responding to events triggered by the user or the server. It's responsible for:
   - Receiving events (like clicks, form submissions, or custom events).
   - Updating the socket's state based on the event.
   - Optionally performing actions like saving data to the database or sending messages.
4. **Update:** This stage is like making adjustments during the performance based on audience feedback. The update function is called after handle_event and allows you to:
   - Make further modifications to the socket's state.
   - This can be useful for separating concerns or applying common logic after different events.
5. **Render:** This is the grand finale, where the LiveView presents its updated state to the audience. The render function takes the socket's state and transforms it into HTML. This HTML is then sent to the browser, where LiveView efficiently patches it into the existing page.

Visualizing the Flow:

It can be helpful to visualize the LiveView lifecycle as a flow chart:

Mount -> Handle Params -> Render -> (Handle Event -> Update -> Render)*

The (Handle Event -> Update -> Render)* part indicates that the handle event, update, and render cycle can repeat multiple times as the user interacts with the page.

Let's Get Practical:

Let's create a simple LiveView that demonstrates the lifecycle stages.

1. **Create a new Phoenix project:** If you haven't already, create a new project:

Bash

```
mix phx.new my_lifecycle_app
cd my_lifecycle_app
```

2. **Create a LiveView:** Generate a LiveView module named LifecycleLive:

Bash

```
mix phx.gen.live Lifecycle lifecycle
```

3. **Update the LiveView module:** Replace the contents of lifecycle_live.ex with the following:

Elixir

```elixir
defmodule MyLifecycleAppWeb.LifecycleLive do
use MyLifecycleAppWeb, :live_view
def mount(_params, _session, socket) do
IO.puts "Mount called"
{:ok, assign(socket, count: 0, message: "Initial message")}
end
def handle_params(params, _url, socket) do
IO.puts "Handle params called with params: #{inspect(params)}"
{:noreply, assign(socket, message: "Params updated!")}
end
def handle_event("increment", _value, socket) do
IO.puts "Increment event handled"
{:noreply, update(socket, :count, &(&1 + 1))}
end
def handle_event("change_message", _value, socket) do
IO.puts "Change message event handled"
{:noreply, assign(socket, message: "Message changed!")}
end
def update(assigns, socket) do
IO.puts "Update called"
{:ok, assign(socket, assigns)}
end
def render(assigns) do
IO.puts "Render called"
~L"""
```

```
<div>
Count: <%= @count %>
<button phx-click="increment">Increment</button>
<button          phx-click="change_message">Change
Message</button>
<p><%= @message %></p>
</div>
"""

end
end
```

4. **Define the route:** Open the router file (lib/my_lifecycle_app_web/router.ex) and add a route for LifecycleLive:

Elixir

```
scope "/", MyLifecycleAppWeb do
pipe_through :browser
live "/lifecycle", LifecycleLive
end
```

5. **Start the server:** Run mix phx.server in your terminal.
6. **Visit the page:** Open your browser and go to http://localhost:4000/lifecycle.

Observe the Output:

Observe the output in your terminal. You'll see the following messages:

Mount called
Handle params called with params: %{}
Render called

This shows the initial lifecycle stages. Now, click the "Increment" button and observe the output:

Increment event handled
Update called
Render called

This shows the handle_event, update, and render cycle. Click the "Change Message" button to see the same cycle with a different event.

This example demonstrates the LiveView lifecycle in action. By understanding these stages, you can build more complex and interactive LiveView applications with confidence.

5.4 Forms and User Input

Let's talk about how LiveView makes handling forms and user input a breeze! In traditional web applications, dealing with forms often involved writing JavaScript code for validation, error handling, and submitting data to the server. But with LiveView, things get much simpler.

LiveView Forms:

LiveView takes a server-side approach to form handling. Here's the basic idea:

1. **Server-Rendered Form:** The initial form is rendered on the server using Elixir and sent to the browser as HTML.
2. **Real-time Interaction:** As the user interacts with the form (typing, selecting options, etc.), LiveView sends these changes to the server in real-time.
3. **Server-Side Validation:** The server validates the input data using Elixir's powerful pattern matching and validation capabilities.
4. **Dynamic Updates:** If there are validation errors, the server re-renders the form with error messages, providing instant feedback to the user.
5. **Form Submission:** When the user submits the form, LiveView handles the submission, processes the data, and updates the page accordingly.

The Benefits:

This server-side approach offers several advantages:

- **Less JavaScript:** You can handle form validation and submission with minimal or no JavaScript.
- **Real-time Feedback:** Users get instant feedback on their input, making the experience smoother and more intuitive.
- **Secure Validation:** Validation happens on the server, ensuring data integrity and security.
- **Simplified Development:** You can leverage Elixir's powerful features for handling and validating data.

Let's Get Practical:

Let's create a user registration form using LiveView to see how it handles user input and validation.

1. **Create a new Phoenix project:** If you haven't already, create a new project:

Bash

```
mix phx.new my_form_app
cd my_form_app
```

2. **Generate a User context:** We'll need a context to manage users and a schema to define the user data:

Bash

```
mix phx.gen.html Accounts User users name:string email:string
mix phx.gen.context Accounts User users name:string email:string
```

3. **Migrate the database:** Run the migrations to create the users table:

Bash

```
mix ecto.migrate
```

4. **Create a LiveView:** Generate a LiveView module named UserRegistrationLive:

Bash

```
mix       phx.gen.live      Accounts      UserRegistration
user_registration
```

5. **Update the LiveView module:** Open the generated LiveView file (**lib/my_form_app_web/live/accounts/user_regist ration_live.ex**) and update it:

Elixir

```
defmodule MyFormAppWeb.Accounts.UserRegistrationLive
do
use MyFormAppWeb, :live_view
alias MyFormApp.Accounts
def mount(_params, _session, socket) do
{:ok,                 assign(socket,                changeset:
Accounts.change_user(%Accounts.User{}))}
end

def render(assigns) do
~L"""
<.form let={f} for={@changeset} phx-submit="save">
<%= if @changeset.action do %>
<div class="alert alert-danger">
<p>Oops, something went wrong![1] Please check the errors
below.</p>
</div>
<% end %>
<%= label f, :name %>
<%= text_input f, :name %>
<%= error_tag f, :name %>
<%= label f, :email %>
```

89

```
<%= text_input f, :email %>
<%= error_tag f, :email² %>
<%= submit "Register" %>
</.form>
"""

end
def handle_event("save", %{"user" => user_params},
socket) do
case Accounts.create_user(user_params) do
{:ok, user} ->
{:noreply,
socket
|> put_flash(:info, "User created³ successfully.")
|> redirect(to: Routes.user_path(socket, :show, user))}
{:error, %Ecto.Changeset{} = changeset} ->
{:noreply, assign(socket, changeset: changeset)}
end
end
end
```

6. **Define the route:** Open the router file (**lib/my_form_app_web/router.ex**) and add a route for **UserRegistrationLive** within the scope **"/"**, **MyFormAppWeb** block:

Elixir

```
live "/users/new", Accounts.UserRegistrationLive, :new
```

7. **Start the server:** Run **mix phx.server** to start the server.

8. **Visit the page:** Open your browser and go to http://localhost:4000/users/new.

You should see a user registration form. Try submitting the form with invalid data (e.g., an empty name or an invalid email format). You'll see error messages appear in real-time without any page reloads!

Code Breakdown: Understanding the Form Handling

- **mount function:** This function sets up the initial form with an empty changeset for a new user.
- **render function:** This function renders the form using the <.form> component, which provides convenient helpers for generating form elements and displaying error messages.
- **phx-submit attribute:** This attribute in the <form> tag tells LiveView to send a "save" event to the server when the form is submitted.
- **handle_event function:** This function handles the "save" event, attempts to create the user, and either redirects to the user's profile page on success or re-renders the form with errors on failure.

This example demonstrates how LiveView simplifies form handling and validation. By leveraging Elixir's capabilities and the real-time nature of LiveView, you can create user-friendly and efficient forms with ease.

Chapter 6: Advanced LiveView Techniques

You've got the basics of LiveView under your belt! Now, let's explore some more advanced techniques that will help you build even more powerful and sophisticated web applications. Think of these as your secret weapons for mastering the art of LiveView development.

6.1 Live Components:

Let's talk about how to write cleaner and more maintainable LiveView code by using LiveComponents! Think of LiveComponents as building blocks for your user interface. They allow you to encapsulate specific UI elements and their associated logic into reusable components, making your code more modular and organized.

Why Use LiveComponents?

Imagine you're building a website with a user profile section that appears on multiple pages (e.g., the homepage, the user's profile page, and a leaderboard). Instead of repeating the same code for displaying the user profile in each LiveView, you can create a UserCard LiveComponent and reuse it across your application.

This brings several benefits:

- **Reusability:** Avoid code duplication and keep your code DRY (Don't Repeat Yourself).

- **Maintainability:** If you need to make changes to the user profile display, you only need to update the UserCard component, not every LiveView that uses it.
- **Modularity:** Components help break down complex UIs into smaller, more manageable pieces.
- **Testability:** You can test components in isolation, making it easier to ensure they function correctly.

Creating a LiveComponent

Let's create a simple **UserCard** LiveComponent that displays a user's name, email, and avatar.

1. **Generate the component:** In your Phoenix project, run the following command:

Bash

```
mix phx.gen.live_component UserCard user_card
```

This creates a LiveComponent module named **UserCard** and a corresponding template file (**user_card_component.ex** and **user_card_component.html.leex**).

2. **Update the component module:** Open the generated **user_card_component.ex** file and update the **render** function:

Elixir

```
defmodule MyLiveviewAppWeb.UserCardComponent do
use MyLiveviewAppWeb, :live_component
def render(assigns) do
```

```
~L"""
<div class="user-card">
<img    src="<%=    @user.avatar_url   %>"   alt="<%=
@user.name %>">
<h3><%= @user.name %></h3>
<p><%= @user.email %></p>
</div>
"""
end
end
```

Using the LiveComponent

Now, you can use this **UserCardComponent** in your
LiveViews.

Elixir

```
# In your LiveView template
<.live_component
module={MyLiveviewAppWeb.UserCardComponent}
id="user-card" user={@user} />
```

Passing Data to the Component

You can pass data to the component using assigns. In the
example above, we pass the @user assign to the
component. This allows you to customize the component's
behavior and appearance based on the data passed to it.

Component Lifecycle

LiveComponents have a similar lifecycle to LiveViews,
including mount and update functions. You can use these

functions to initialize the component's state and handle updates.

Example with Lifecycle Methods

Elixir

```elixir
defmodule MyLiveviewAppWeb.UserCardComponent do
use MyLiveviewAppWeb, :live_component
def mount(socket) do
{:ok, assign(socket, show_details: false)}
end
def update(assigns, socket) do
{:ok, assign(socket, assigns)}
end
def render(assigns) do
~L"""
<div class="user-card">
<img src="<%= @user.avatar_url %>" alt="<%= @user.name %>">
<h3><%= @user.name %></h3>
<p><%= @user.email %></p>
<%= if @show_details do %>
<p>More details about the user...</p>
<% end %>
<button phx-click="toggle_details">Toggle Details</button>
</div>
"""
end
def handle_event("toggle_details", _value, socket) do
{:noreply, update(socket, :show_details, &(!&1))}
end
```

end

In this example, the component manages its internal state (show_details) and handles the "toggle_details" event to show or hide additional user details.

By using LiveComponents effectively, you can create modular, reusable, and maintainable UI elements that enhance the structure and organization of your LiveView applications.

6.2 Live Navigation:

Okay, let's talk about how LiveView makes navigating between different parts of your application smooth and efficient! Traditionally, navigating between pages involved full page reloads, which could be jarring and slow. But with LiveView's **live navigation** features, you can update the URL and switch between LiveViews without those clunky full page refreshes.

The Power of Client-Side Routing

LiveView offers two primary functions for client-side routing:

- live_patch: This function is like a subtle scene change. It updates the URL and parameters of the *current* LiveView without reloading the entire page. This is great for situations where you want to update the content dynamically based on user interaction (e.g., filtering a list, changing tabs, or updating a view).
- live_redirect: This function is like a complete scene change. It redirects to a *different* LiveView, effectively

mounting a new LiveView while keeping the existing LiveView connection alive. This is useful for navigating between different sections of your application (e.g., going from the homepage to a product page).

Why Live Navigation Matters

Live navigation brings several benefits to your LiveView applications:

- **Speed and Efficiency:** Avoids full page reloads, making navigation faster and smoother.
- **State Preservation:** LiveViews can preserve their state between navigations, providing a more seamless user experience.
- **SEO Friendliness:** Updates the URL in the browser's address bar, making it easier for search engines to index your content and for users to share links.

Let's Get Practical:

Let's create a simple tabbed interface using live_patch to demonstrate live navigation.

1. **Create a new Phoenix project:** If you haven't already, create a new project:

Bash

```
mix phx.new my_navigation_app
cd my_navigation_app
```

2. **Create a LiveView:** Generate a LiveView module named **TabNavigationLive**:

Bash

```
mix phx.gen.live TabNavigation tab_navigation
```

3. **Update the LiveView module:** Open the generated tab_navigation_live.ex file and update it:

Elixir

```
defmodule MyNavigationAppWeb.TabNavigationLive do
use MyNavigationAppWeb, :live_view
def mount(_params, _session, socket) do
{:ok, assign(socket, current_tab: "home")}
end
def handle_params(params, _url, socket) do
{:noreply, assign(socket, current_tab: params["tab"] ||
"home")}
end
def render(assigns) do
~L"""
<div>
<nav>
        <%= live_patch "Home", to:
Routes.tab_navigation_path(@socket, :index, tab:
"home"), class: ("active" if @current_tab == "home")
%>
        <%= live_patch "Profile", to:
Routes.tab_navigation_path(@socket, :index, tab:
```

```
"profile"), class: ("active" if @current_tab == "profile")
%>
          <%=        live_patch        "Settings",        to:
Routes.tab_navigation_path(@socket,      :index,      tab:
"settings"),   class:   ("active"   if   @current_tab   ==
"settings") %>
    </nav>
<div id="tab-content">
<%= if @current_tab == "home" do %>
<p>Welcome to the home tab!</p>
 <% end %>
<%= if @current_tab == "profile" do %>
<p>This is your profile page.</p>
<% end %>
<%= if @current_tab == "settings" do %>
<p>Adjust your settings here.</p>
<% end %>
</div>
</div>
"""

end
end
```

4. **Define the route:** Open the router file (lib/my_navigation_app_web/router.ex) and add a route for TabNavigationLive:

Elixir

```
scope "/", MyNavigationAppWeb do
pipe_through :browser
```

```
live "/tabs", TabNavigationLive
end
```

5. **Start the server:** Run `mix phx.server` in your terminal.
6. **Visit the page:** Open your browser and go to http://localhost:4000/tabs.

You should see a tabbed interface with three tabs (Home, Profile, Settings). Click on the tabs to navigate between them. Notice how the content changes without a full page reload!

Code Breakdown: Understanding the Navigation

- **mount function:** Initializes the current_tab to "home".
- **handle_params function:** Updates the current_tab based on the tab parameter in the URL.
- **live_patch functions:** These functions generate links that update the URL with the corresponding tab parameter and trigger the handle_params function.
- **Conditional rendering:** The if blocks in the template render the appropriate content based on the current_tab.

This example demonstrates how live_patch enables seamless client-side navigation in LiveView. By using live_patch **and** live_redirect effectively, you can create smooth and efficient navigation experiences in your web applications.

6.3 Testing LiveViews

Alright, let's talk about how to make sure your LiveViews are rock-solid and bug-free! Testing is an essential part of software development, and LiveViews are no exception. Phoenix provides excellent tools and functions specifically designed for testing LiveViews, making it easier to ensure your interactive components behave as expected.

Why Test LiveViews?

Testing your LiveViews offers several benefits:

- **Catch Bugs Early:** Tests help you identify and fix bugs early in the development process, saving you time and headaches down the road.
- **Ensure Correctness:** Tests verify that your LiveViews render the correct HTML, update their state correctly, and handle events as expected.
- **Confidence in Refactoring:** When you refactor or make changes to your code, tests provide a safety net, ensuring you haven't introduced any regressions.
- **Documentation:** Well-written tests can serve as documentation, demonstrating how your LiveViews are intended to work.

Testing Tools: live Function and Assertions

Phoenix provides a handy live function for testing LiveViews. This function allows you to mount a LiveView in a test environment and interact with it programmatically.

Here's the basic structure of a LiveView test:

Elixir

```
test "my LiveView test", %{conn: conn} do
{:ok,          view,          html}          =          live(conn,
MyLiveviewAppWeb.MyLiveView)
# Assertions about the initial HTML
assert html =~ "Expected content"
# Simulate user interactions
view
|> element("button")
|> render_click()
# Assertions about the updated HTML or state
assert view
|> render() =~ "Updated content"
end
```

Let's break it down:

- **live(conn, MyLiveviewAppWeb.MyLiveView)**: This mounts the **MyLiveView** LiveView and returns a tuple containing the **view**, which is a struct representing the LiveView process, and the **html**, which is the initial HTML rendered by the LiveView.
- **element("button")**: This selects an element (in this case, a button) within the LiveView's HTML.
- **render_click()**: This simulates a click on the selected element, triggering any associated events and updating the LiveView's state.
- **render()**: This re-renders the LiveView's HTML after the simulated interaction.
- **assert macros**: These are used to make assertions about the LiveView's behavior, such as checking the rendered HTML or the LiveView's internal state.

Let's Get Practical:

Let's write some tests for the **CounterLive** we created earlier.

1. **Create a test file:** In your my_liveview_app_test/my_liveview_app_web/live_test/ directory, create a file named counter_live_test.ex.
2. **Write the tests:** Add the following code to counter_live_test.ex:

Elixir

```elixir
defmodule MyLiveviewAppWeb.LiveTest.CounterLiveTest do
use MyLiveviewAppWeb.ConnCase
import Phoenix.LiveViewTest
test "counter increments on click", %{conn: conn} do
{:ok, view, html} = live(conn, MyLiveviewAppWeb.CounterLive)
assert html =~ "Count: 0"
view
|> element("button")
|> render_click()
assert view
|> render() =~ "Count: 1"
end
end
```

3. **Run the tests:** In your terminal, run mix test.

You should see the test pass, indicating that the CounterLive correctly increments the count when the button is clicked.

Testing Different Scenarios

You can write tests for various scenarios, such as:

- **Initial rendering:** Verify that the LiveView renders the correct initial HTML.
- **Event handling:** Test that the LiveView handles different events correctly.
- **State updates:** Check that the LiveView updates its state as expected in response to events.
- **Form submissions:** Test form submissions and validation.

By writing comprehensive tests for your LiveViews, you can ensure they are robust, reliable, and behave as intended. This gives you confidence in your code and helps you deliver high-quality web applications.

6.4 Optimizing LiveView Performance

Alright, let's talk about making your LiveViews lightning fast! While LiveView is generally quite performant out of the box, there are some techniques you can use to squeeze out even more speed and efficiency, especially for complex LiveViews or high-traffic situations. Think of this as fine-tuning your LiveView engine to achieve peak performance.

Why Optimize?

Optimizing your LiveView performance can lead to:

- **Faster Page Loads:** Users get a snappier and more responsive experience.
- **Reduced Server Load:** Your server can handle more users and traffic with the same resources.
- **Lower Costs:** If you're paying for server resources, optimizing performance can help you save money.
- **Happy Users:** Everyone loves a fast and smooth web experience!

Optimization Techniques: Fine-Tuning Your LiveView

Here are some key strategies for optimizing LiveView performance:

1. Minimize Updates: Avoid Unnecessary Re-renders

LiveView automatically re-renders the parts of the page that are affected by changes in the socket's assigns. However, sometimes you might want to prevent certain parts from re-rendering unnecessarily. You can achieve this using the phx-update attribute.

- **phx-update="ignore":** This tells LiveView to completely ignore updates for this part of the DOM.

HTML

```
<div id="static-content" phx-update="ignore">
This content will not be re-rendered.
</div>
```

- **phx-update="append"**: This is useful for lists. It tells LiveView to append new items to the list instead of re-rendering the entire list.

HTML

```
<ul id="my-list" phx-update="append">
<%= for item <- @items do %>
<li><%= item %></li>
<% end %>
</ul>
```

2. Optimize Data Fetching:

When fetching data from the database, be mindful of the following:

- **Fetch Only What You Need:** Don't retrieve more data than necessary. Use Ecto's query functions to select only the required fields and filter the results effectively.
- **Efficient Queries**: Use Ecto's preload function to avoid N+1 queries when fetching associated data. Optimize your database queries by adding indexes and using appropriate data types.

3. Caching: Store Frequently Accessed Data

Caching can significantly improve performance by storing frequently accessed data in memory, reducing the need to hit the database repeatedly.

- **ETS (Erlang Term Storage):** ETS is an in-memory key-value store that's perfect for caching data in Elixir applications.
- **Phoenix.PubSub:** You can use Phoenix.PubSub to cache data that needs to be shared across multiple LiveViews.

4. Asynchronous Tasks: Offload Long-Running Operations

If you have long-running operations (e.g., sending emails, processing images, making external API calls), offload them to background processes using **Task.async**. This prevents them from blocking the main LiveView process and keeps the UI responsive.

Elixir

```elixir
def handle_event("submit", _value, socket) do
Task.async(fn ->
# Perform long-running operation here
end)
{:noreply, socket}
end
```

5. Temporary Assigns:

For LiveViews that handle large or frequently changing data, temporary assigns can help reduce memory usage. Temporary assigns are reset to their default value after every render, preventing stale data from accumulating in memory.

Elixir

```elixir
def mount(_params, _session, socket) do
```

```
{:ok, assign(socket,
items: [],
temporary_assigns: [items: []]
)}
end
```

Let's Get Practical:

Let's take an example of a LiveView that displays a list of products fetched from the database.

Elixir

```
defmodule MyLiveviewAppWeb.ProductListLive do
use MyLiveviewAppWeb, :live_view
alias MyLiveviewApp.Products
def mount(_params, _session, socket) do
{:ok, assign(socket, products: Products.list_products())}
end
def render(assigns) do
~L"""
<ul>
<%= for product <- @products do %>
<li><%= product.name %> - <%= product.price %></li>
<% end %>
</ul>
"""
end
end
```

Optimization Steps

1. **phx-update="append":**   Add   the
   phx-update="append" attribute to the <ul> tag to
   optimize list updates.
2. **Temporary Assigns:** Make the **products** assign
   temporary to reduce memory usage:

Elixir

```elixir
def mount(_params, _session, socket) do
{:ok, assign(socket,
products: Products.list_products(),
temporary_assigns: [products: []]
)}
end
```

3. **Asynchronous Task (if applicable):** If fetching
   products is a long-running operation, move it to an
   asynchronous task.

By applying these optimization techniques, you can ensure
your LiveView applications are fast, efficient, and provide a
delightful user experience. Remember to profile and
measure your performance to identify bottlenecks and
focus your optimization efforts where they'll have the
greatest impact.

Chapter 7: JavaScript Interoperability

Let's talk about how Elixir and JavaScript can work together in your LiveView applications! While LiveView aims to minimize the amount of JavaScript you need to write, there are still situations where you might want to leverage JavaScript's capabilities for specific tasks. This chapter explores how to bridge the gap between Elixir and JavaScript, allowing them to communicate and cooperate seamlessly.

7.1 Calling JavaScript from Elixir

Let's explore how you can sprinkle some JavaScript magic into your LiveView applications directly from your Elixir code! While LiveView aims to minimize the amount of JavaScript you need to write, there are times when JavaScript's DOM manipulation prowess or its ability to interact with browser APIs comes in handy.

The JS Module: Your Elixir-to-JavaScript Translator

LiveView provides a handy tool called the Phoenix.LiveView.JS module. This module acts like a translator, allowing you to write JavaScript commands in your Elixir code that will be sent to the browser and executed there.

Why Call JavaScript from Elixir?

Here are a few scenarios where calling JavaScript from Elixir can be useful:

- **Visual Effects and Animations:** You might want to trigger a cool animation or visual effect when something happens in your LiveView, like a new item being added to a list or a form being submitted successfully.
- **Browser APIs:** You might need to interact with a browser API, like the Geolocation API to get the user's location, or the Notification API to display a notification.
- **Third-Party JavaScript Libraries:** You might want to use a JavaScript library for specific functionality, like a charting library or a date picker.
- **Fine-grained DOM Manipulation:** While LiveView handles most DOM updates efficiently, there might be cases where you need more fine-grained control over DOM elements, and JavaScript is excellent for that.

How it Works: Sending Commands to the Browser

When you use the **JS** module in your LiveView, it generates JavaScript commands that are sent to the browser over the LiveView WebSocket connection. These commands are then executed in the browser's JavaScript environment.

Let's Get Practical:

Let's create a simple example where we trigger a JavaScript alert from our LiveView.

1. **Create a new LiveView:** In your Phoenix project, generate a new LiveView called **JSExampleLive:**

Bash

```
mix phx.gen.live JSExample js_example
```

2. **Update the LiveView module:** Open the generated js_example_live.ex file and update it as follows:

Elixir

```elixir
defmodule MyLiveviewAppWeb.JSExampleLive do
use MyLiveviewAppWeb, :live_view
def mount(_params, _session, socket) do
{:ok, assign(socket, :message, "Hello from Elixir!")}
end
def render(assigns) do
~L"""
<button phx-click="show_alert">Show Alert</button>
"""
end
def handle_event("show_alert", _value, socket) d
{:noreply, push_event(socket, "show_alert", %{message:
"Hello from Elixir!"})}
end
end
```

3. **Update the template file:** Open the generated template file (js_example_live.html.leex) and add this script tag within the <body> tags:

HTML

```html
<script>
window.addEventListener('phx:show_alert', (e) => {
alert(e.detail.message);
});
```

```
</script>
```

4. This script listens for a custom event called **phx:show_alert** that will be pushed from the LiveView. When the event is received, it displays an alert with the message received from the server.

5. **Update the router:** Open your **router.ex** file and add a route for the **JSExampleLive**:

Elixir

live "/js_example", JSExampleLive

6. **Start the server:** Run **mix phx.server** in your terminal.

7. **Visit the page:** Open your browser and go to **http://localhost:4000/js_example**.

You should see a button labeled "Show Alert". When you click the button, a JavaScript alert will pop up with the message "Hello from Elixir!".

Code Breakdown:

- **phx-click="show_alert":** This attribute in the button tells LiveView to send a "show_alert" event to the server when the button is clicked.
- **handle_event("show_alert", _value, socket):** This function in the LiveView handles the "show_alert" event.
- **JS.push("show_alert", %{"message" => socket.assigns.message}):** This line uses the JS

module to generate a JavaScript command that pushes the "show_alert" event with the message to the client.

- **alert(message):** The JavaScript code in the template listens for the "show_alert" event and displays an alert with the received message.

This example demonstrates how you can use the JS module to trigger JavaScript code from your LiveView. You can explore the different functions provided by the JS module (like **add_class**, **remove_class**, **show**, **hide**, etc.) to perform various DOM manipulations and interact with browser APIs.

7.2 Calling Elixir from JavaScript

Alright, let's turn the tables and see how you can make JavaScript talk to your Elixir LiveView! While LiveView primarily handles the heavy lifting on the server, there are situations where you might want to trigger actions in your Elixir code based on events that happen in the browser. This is where calling Elixir from JavaScript comes into play.

Why Call Elixir from JavaScript?

Here are a few scenarios where calling Elixir from JavaScript can be beneficial:

- **Client-Side Events:** You might have events that originate in the browser that you want to handle on the server. For example, you might want to track user interactions like mouse movements, scroll events, or window resizes.

- **Browser API Interactions**: When interacting with certain browser APIs, you might need to send data back to the server. For example, if you're using the Geolocation API to get the user's location, you might want to send the location data to your LiveView for processing or storage.
- **Third-Party Library Integration**: If you're using a JavaScript library that emits events, you might want to send those events to your LiveView.

How it Works: Sending Messages over the WebSocket

LiveView establishes a persistent WebSocket connection between the browser and the server. This connection allows for bidirectional communication, meaning you can send messages from the client (JavaScript) to the server (Elixir) and vice versa.

The pushEvent Function:

Within your LiveView's JavaScript hook, you have access to a pushEvent function. This function allows you to send events to your LiveView on the server.

Here's the basic syntax:

JavaScript

```javascript
this.pushEvent("my_event", { some: "data" });
```

This code sends an event named "my_event" to the server, along with any data you want to include in the event.

Handling Events in Elixir:

On the Elixir side, you handle these events using the familiar **handle_event** function in your LiveView.

Elixir

```
def handle_event("my_event", %{"some" => data},
socket) do
# Process the event and update the socket's state
end
```

Let's Get Practical:

Let's create a simple example where we send a message from the browser to the LiveView using JavaScript.

1. **Create a new LiveView:** In your Phoenix project, generate a new LiveView called **ClientEventLive**:

Bash

```
mix phx.gen.live ClientEvent client_event
```

2. **Update the LiveView module:** Open the generated client_event_live.ex file and update it:

Elixir

```
defmodule MyLiveviewAppWeb.ClientEventLive do
use MyLiveviewAppWeb, :live_view
def mount(_params, _session, socket) do
{:ok, assign(socket, :message, "No message yet")}
end
def render(assigns) do
```

```
~L"""
<div id="message-container"><%= @message %></div>
<button                 phx-click="send_message">Send
Message</button>
"""
end
def handle_event("send_message", _value, socket) do
{:noreply, push_event(socket, "send_message")}
end
def handle_event("receive_message", %{"message" =>
message}, socket) do
{:noreply, assign(socket, :message, message)}
end
end
```

3. **Update the template file:** Open the generated template file (**client_event_live.html.leex**) and add this script tag within the <body> tags:

HTML

```
<script>
window.addEventListener('phx:send_message', (e) => {
let liveSocket = new LiveSocket("/live", Socket, {
params: {_csrf_token: csrfToken}
});
liveSocket.connect();
let message = prompt("Enter a message to send to the
server:");
if (message) {
liveSocket.pushEvent("receive_message",  {  message:
message });
```

```
}
});
</script>
```

This script listens for a custom event called phx:send_message that will be pushed from the LiveView. When the event is received, it prompts the user for a message and sends it to the server using liveSocket.pushEvent.

4. **Update the router:** Open your **router.ex** file and add a route for the **ClientEventLive**:

Elixir

live "/client_event", ClientEventLive

5. **Start the server:** Run **mix phx.server** in your terminal.
6. **Visit the page:** Open your browser and go to **http://localhost:4000/client_event**.

You should see a button labeled "Send Message". When you click the button, you'll be prompted to enter a message. After entering the message, it will be sent to the LiveView and displayed on the page.

Code Breakdown: The Communication Flow

- **phx-click="send_message":** This attribute in the button triggers the "send_message" event in the LiveView.

- handle_event("send_message", _value, socket): This function in the LiveView handles the "send_message" event and pushes a "send_message" event to the client.
- window.addEventListener('phx:send_message', ...): This JavaScript code listens for the "send_message" event from the server.
- liveSocket.pushEvent("receive_message", { message: message }): This sends the "receive_message" event with the user's message to the LiveView.
- handle_event("receive_message", %{"message" => message}, socket): This function in the LiveView handles the "receive_message" event and updates the message assign.

This example demonstrates how you can establish communication from JavaScript to your Elixir LiveView, allowing you to respond to client-side events and trigger server-side actions.

7.3 Building LiveView Components with JavaScript

Let's take things up a notch and see how you can combine the power of Elixir and JavaScript to build custom LiveView components! This is where the real magic happens, allowing you to create interactive UI elements that leverage the strengths of both languages.

Why Build Components with JavaScript?

While LiveView excels at handling most UI interactions, there are situations where JavaScript's capabilities shine:

- **Complex UI Interactions:** For components with intricate behaviors or animations that might be challenging to implement solely with LiveView, JavaScript can provide more fine-grained control.
- **Third-Party Library Integration:** If you want to integrate a JavaScript library that provides specific UI functionality (e.g., a charting library, a rich text editor, or a drag-and-drop interface), you can wrap it within a LiveView component.
- **Reusability:** By encapsulating JavaScript functionality within a LiveView component, you can easily reuse it across your application.

The Approach: A Collaborative Effort

Building LiveView components with JavaScript involves a collaborative approach:

1. **Elixir Structure:** You define the component's structure and behavior using Elixir and LiveView.
2. **JavaScript Functionality:** You implement the component's interactive logic using JavaScript.
3. **Communication Bridge:** You use JS commands and pushEvent to establish communication between Elixir and JavaScript.

Let's Get Practical:

Let's create a tooltip component that displays a helpful message when the user hovers over an element.

1. **Generate the component:** In your Phoenix project, run:

Bash

```
mix phx.gen.live_component Tooltip tooltip
```

2. **Update the component module:** Open the generated **tooltip_component.ex** file and update it:

Elixir

```
defmodule MyLiveviewAppWeb.TooltipComponent do
use MyLiveviewAppWeb, :live_component
def render(assigns) do
~L"""
<span id="<%= @id %>" class="tooltip-container" phx-hook="Tooltip">
<%= @inner_block %>
<span class="tooltip-text"><%= @text %></span>
</span>
"""
end
end
```

3. **Add JavaScript hook:** In your **app.js** file, add the following JavaScript code:

JavaScript

```
let Hooks = {};
```

```
Hooks.Tooltip = {
mounted() {
this.el.addEventListener("mouseover", () => {
this.el.querySelector(".tooltip-text").style.visibility        =
"visible";
});
this.el.addEventListener("mouseout", () => {
this.el.querySelector(".tooltip-text").style.visibility        =
"hidden";
});
}
};
let liveSocket = new LiveSocket("/live", Socket, {
params: {_csrf_token: csrfToken},
hooks: Hooks
});
liveSocket.connect();
```

4. **Use the component in your LiveView:**

Elixir

```
<.live_component
module={MyLiveviewAppWeb.TooltipComponent}
id="my-tooltip" text="This is a tooltip!">
 Hover over me
</.live_component>
```

Code Breakdown:

- **Elixir Component:** The **TooltipComponent** defines the structure of the tooltip with a container and a tooltip text element.
- **JavaScript Hook:** The Tooltip JavaScript hook adds event listeners for **mouseover** and **mouseout** to control the visibility of the tooltip text.
- **Communication:** The **phx-hook="Tooltip"** attribute in the component's template connects the Elixir component with the JavaScript hook.

Now, when you run your Phoenix application and hover over the "Hover over me" text, you'll see the tooltip appear!

This example demonstrates how to build a LiveView component that leverages JavaScript for interactive behavior. By combining the strengths of both Elixir and JavaScript, you can create reusable and engaging UI elements that enhance your LiveView applications.

Chapter 8: Integrating Frontend Frameworks

Let's explore how to bring the best of both worlds into your LiveView applications by integrating popular frontend frameworks! While LiveView provides a powerful way to build dynamic interfaces with Elixir, there might be situations where you want to leverage the features and ecosystems of JavaScript frameworks like React, Vue, or Alpine.js. This chapter shows you how to seamlessly blend these frameworks with your LiveView projects.

8.1 Using JavaScript Libraries

Alright, let's talk about how to supercharge your LiveView applications by tapping into the vast world of JavaScript libraries! While LiveView is awesome for building dynamic interfaces, sometimes you need specialized tools or functionalities that are readily available in JavaScript libraries. This is where knowing how to integrate those libraries seamlessly comes in handy.

Why Use JavaScript Libraries?

JavaScript has a massive ecosystem of libraries that can provide solutions for almost any frontend need. Here are a few reasons why you might want to use them in your LiveView projects:

- **Specialized Functionality:** Need interactive charts? A slick date picker? Smooth animations? There's likely a JavaScript library out there that does exactly what you need.

- **UI Components:** Many libraries offer pre-built UI components like modals, carousels, and tooltips, saving you the time and effort of building them from scratch.
- **Utilities:** Libraries like Lodash or Moment.js provide helpful utility functions for working with arrays, objects, dates, and other common tasks.
- **Community and Support:** Popular JavaScript libraries have large communities and extensive documentation, making it easier to find solutions and get help when needed.

Integrating a JavaScript Library: A Step-by-Step Guide

Here's a general approach to integrating a JavaScript library into your LiveView application:

1. **Install the Library:** Use npm (Node Package Manager) or yarn to install the library. Open your terminal, navigate to your Phoenix project's root directory, and run:

Bash

```
npm install library-name
# Example: npm install chart.js
```

2. **Import the Library:** In your assets/js/app.js file (or wherever you manage your JavaScript code), import the library using the import statement:

JavaScript

```javascript
import Something from 'library-name';
// Example: import Chart from 'chart.js/auto';
```

3. **Use the Library in Your LiveView:** In your LiveView template, you can now use the library within a <script> tag.

Elixir

```elixir
def render(assigns) do
  ~L"""
  <div id="my-chart"></div>
  <script>
  // JavaScript code using the library
  let myChart = new Something( /* ... configuration ... */ );
  </script>
  """
end
```

Let's Get Practical: Adding Interactive Charts with Chart.js

Let's add a dynamic bar chart to a LiveView using the popular Chart.js library.

1. **Install Chart.js:**

Bash

```bash
npm install chart.js
```

2. **Create a LiveView:** Generate a new LiveView named ChartLive:

Bash

mix phx.gen.live Chart chart

3. **Update the LiveView:** Open the generated chart_live.ex file and update it as follows:

Elixir

```elixir
defmodule MyLiveviewAppWeb.ChartLive do
use MyLiveviewAppWeb, :live_view
def mount(_params, _session, socket) do
{:ok, assign(socket, :chart_data, %{
labels: ["Red", "Blue", "Yellow", "Green", "Purple", "Orange"],
datasets: [%{
label: "# of Votes",
data: [12, 19, 3, 5, 2, 3],
backgroundColor: [
'rgba(255, 99, 132, 0.2)',
'rgba(54, 162, 235, 0.2)',
'rgba(255, 206, 86, 0.2)',
'rgba(75, 192, 192, 0.2)',
'rgba(153, 102, 255, 0.2)',
'rgba(255, 159, 64, 0.2)'
],
borderColor: [
'rgba(255, 99, 132, 1)',
'rgba(54, 162, 235, 1)',
```

```
'rgba(255, 206, 86, 1)',
'rgba(75, 192, 192, 1)',
'rgba(153, 102, 255, 1)',
'rgba(255, 159, 64, 1)'
],
borderWidth: 1
}]
}})}
end
def render(assigns) do
~L"""
<canvas id="myChart"></canvas>
<script>
var                          ctx                          =
document.getElementById('myChart').getContext('2d');
var myChart = new Chart(ctx, {
type: 'bar',
data: <%= Jason.encode!(@chart_data) %>,
options: {
scales: {
y: {
beginAtZero: true
}
}
}
});
</script>
"""
end
end
```

This LiveView defines some sample chart data and renders a <canvas> element where the chart will be drawn. The <script> tag uses Chart.js to create a new chart with the provided data.

4. **Update the router:** Open your router.ex file and add a route for the ChartLive:

Elixir

```
live "/chart", ChartLive
```

5. **Start the server:** Run mix phx.server in your terminal.
6. **Visit the page:** Open your browser and go to http://localhost:4000/chart.

You should see a beautiful bar chart rendered using Chart.js!

This example demonstrates how to integrate a JavaScript library to add interactive elements to your LiveView application. By following this approach, you can leverage the vast ecosystem of JavaScript libraries to enhance your LiveView projects with specialized functionalities and rich user experiences.

8.2 Building Hybrid Applications

Let's explore the exciting world of hybrid applications with LiveView! This is where you can truly blend the strengths of

Elixir and JavaScript frameworks like React, Vue, or Angular to create powerful and versatile web experiences. Think of it like assembling a superhero team, each member bringing their unique skills to the table.

Why Build Hybrid Applications?

There are several reasons why you might choose a hybrid approach:

- **Leverage Existing Expertise:** If you have a team with expertise in a particular JavaScript framework, you can leverage their skills while still benefiting from LiveView's real-time capabilities and server-side rendering.
- **Complex UI Interactions:** For parts of your application that require highly interactive and complex UI elements, a JavaScript framework might offer a more mature ecosystem and tools.
- **Ecosystem and Community:** JavaScript frameworks have vast ecosystems of libraries, tools, and community support that you can tap into.
- **Gradual Adoption:** You can start with a core LiveView application and gradually introduce a JavaScript framework for specific sections or features as needed.

Strategies for Hybrid Bliss

There are a few different strategies for building hybrid applications with LiveView:

- **Islands of Interactivity:** Embed React or Vue components within your LiveView templates for specific interactive sections. This is great for adding framework commitment.

- **Separate Sections:** Divide your application into distinct sections handled by LiveView and sections handled by the JavaScript framework. This allows for clear separation of concerns but requires careful coordination of communication between the sections.
- **Progressive Enhancement:** Start with a core LiveView application and progressively enhance specific parts with a JavaScript framework as needed. This approach prioritizes a solid foundation with LiveView and adds JavaScript framework features strategically.

Let's Get Practical: Integrating a React Component

Let's walk through an example of integrating a simple React component into a LiveView application.

1. **Set up a React Project:** Create a new React project using Create React App. In your terminal, run:

Bash

```
npx create-react-app my-react-app
cd my-react-app
```

2. **Create a Component:** Create a simple React component in src/Greeting.js:

JavaScript

```
import React from 'react';
```

```jsx
function Greeting(props) {
  return <h1>Hello, {props.name}!</h1>;
}

export default Greeting;[1]
```

3. **Build the React App:** Build your React application to generate the production-ready files:

Bash

```bash
npm run build
```

4. **Copy Build Output:** Copy the contents of the **my-react-app/build** directory to your Phoenix app's **priv/static** directory. This makes the React app's assets accessible to your Phoenix application.

5. **Include React Scripts:** In your LiveView template, include the necessary React scripts:

Elixir

```elixir
defmodule MyLiveviewAppWeb.ReactIntegrationLive do
  use MyLiveviewAppWeb, :live_view
  def mount(_params, _session, socket) do
    {:ok, assign(socket, name: "World")}
  end
  def render(assigns) do
    ~L"""
    <div id="react-root"></div>
    <script src="/js/main.js"></script>
```

"""

end

end

6. **Render the React Component:** In your assets/js/app.js file, render the React component:

JavaScript

```javascript
import React from 'react';
import ReactDOM from 'react-dom/client';
import Greeting from './Greeting'; // Assuming Greeting.js
is in the same directory
const root =
ReactDOM.createRoot(document.getElementById('react-r
oot'));
root.render(<Greeting name="World" />);
```

7. **Create and visit the LiveView:** Generate the LiveView and visit the page in your browser.

Bash

```bash
mix phx.gen.live ReactIntegration react_integration
```

8. Update your router.ex to include:

Elixir

```elixir
live "/react_integration", ReactIntegrationLive
```

9. Then, start the server:

Bash

mix phx.server

10. And visit http://localhost:4000/react_integration in your browser.

Now, when you run your Phoenix app, you'll see the React component rendered within your LiveView!

This example demonstrates a basic integration of a React component into a LiveView. You can apply similar principles to integrate other JavaScript frameworks like Vue or Angular. Remember to consider the communication and data flow between your LiveView and the JavaScript framework to ensure a smooth and cohesive user experience.

Chapter 9: Real-time Communication

Get ready to unlock the true power of LiveView with real-time communication! This is where we go beyond simple request-response cycles and build applications that feel truly alive and interconnected. Think of it like upgrading from sending letters to having a live video chat – the difference in immediacy and interactivity is immense.

9.1 Channels and Presence

Phoenix Channels provide the foundation for real-time communication in your LiveView applications. They allow you to create persistent connections between clients and the server, enabling features like chat, collaborative tools, live notifications, and more.onse cycle. Think of it like adding a live chat feature to your website, where users can communicate with each other instantly.

Channels:

Channels are like virtual "rooms" or "topics" where clients (typically web browsers) can connect and communicate with each other in real-time. Each channel has a unique name (the topic) that clients subscribe to. Once subscribed, clients can send and receive messages within that channel, enabling a wide range of real-time interactions.

Why Use Channels?

- **Chat Applications:** Build chat rooms, private messaging, and group conversations.

- **Collaborative Tools:** Create real-time collaborative editing, whiteboarding, or project management tools.[1]
- **Live Notifications:** Send instant notifications to users about events or updates.
- **Multiplayer Games:** Build multiplayer games where players can interact in real-time.[2]
- **Live Dashboards:** Display real-time data updates, such as stock prices, sensor readings, or website analytics.

Presence: Knowing Who's There

Presence adds another layer of real-time awareness to your applications by allowing you to track which users are currently subscribed to a channel.[3] This enables features like:

- **Online/Offline Status:** Show which users are online or offline in real-time.[4]
- **User Lists:** Display a list of users present in a chat room or collaborative space.[5]
- **Real-time Collaboration:** Track who is editing a document or working on a shared task, enabling collaborative features like co-browsing or shared cursors.

Building a Simple Chat Application

Let's build a basic chat application to illustrate how Channels and Presence work together.

1. **Create a New Phoenix Project:**

Bash

```
mix phx.new my_chat_app
cd my_chat_app
```

2. **Generate a Channel:**

Bash

```
mix phx.gen.channel Room
```

3. This generates a **RoomChannel** module and a test file.
4. **Update the Channel:** Open the generated room_channel.ex file and update it as follows:

Elixir

```
defmodule MyChatAppWeb.RoomChannel do
use MyChatAppWeb, :channel
alias MyChatAppWeb.Presence
def join("room:lobby", _payload, socket) do
send(self(), :after_join)
{:ok, socket}
end
def handle_in("new_msg", %{"body" => body}, socket)
do
broadcast! socket, "new_msg", %{body: body,⁶ sender:
socket.assigns.user_name}
{:noreply, socket}
end
def handle_out("new_msg", payload, socket) do
push socket, "new_msg", payload
{:noreply, socket}
end
```

```elixir
defp after_join do
# This is a hack to get the user's name from the session
# In a real application, you would use proper
authentication
user_name                                              =
MyChatAppWeb.Endpoint.broadcast_from!(self(),
"room:lobby", "presence_state", %{})
|> Map.keys()
|> List.first()
|> to_string()
MyChatAppWeb.Endpoint.broadcast_from!(self(),
"room:lobby",  "presence_state",  %{user_name  =>
%{metas: [%{phx_ref: nil}]}})
end
end
```

5. **Update the UserSocket:** Open user_socket.ex and add the channel route:

Elixir

```elixir
## Channels
channel "room:*", MyChatAppWeb.RoomChannel
```

6. **Create a LiveView:** Generate a LiveView called ChatLive:

Bash

```bash
mix phx.gen.live Chat chat
```

7.

8.

9. **Update the LiveView:** Open the generated chat_live.ex file and update it as follows:

Elixir

```elixir
defmodule MyChatAppWeb.ChatLive do
use MyChatAppWeb, :live_view
alias MyChatAppWeb.Presence
def mount(_params, %{"user_name" => user_name},
socket) do
if                    connected?(socket),                    do:
MyChatAppWeb.Endpoint.subscribe("room:lobby")
{:ok,
socket
|> assign(user_name: user_name, message: "",
messages: [], topic: "room:lobby", temporary_assigns:
[messages: []])}
end

def handle_event("new_msg", %{"message" =>
message}, socket) do
MyChatAppWeb.Endpoint.broadcast!(socket.assigns.topic,
"new_msg", %{body: message})
{:noreply, assign(socket, message: "")}
end
def handle_info(%{event: "presence_state", payload:
%{metas: metas}}, socket) do
{:noreply, assign(socket, :presences, metas)}
end
```

```elixir
def handle_info(%{event: "presence_diff", payload: diff}, socket) do
  {:noreply,
  socket
  |> assign(:presences, Presence.update(socket.assigns.presences, diff))
  |> assign(:users, Presence.list(socket.assigns.presences))}
end

def render(assigns) do
  ~L"""
  <div id="chat-container">
  <h2>Welcome to the Chat, <%= @user_name %></h2>
  <div id="users">
  <h3>Online Users:</h3>
  <ul>
  <%= for user <- @users do %>
  <li><%= user.metas |> List.first |> Map.get(:user_name) %></li>
  <% end %>
  </ul>
  </div>
  <div id="chat">
  <h3>Chat Messages:</h3>
  <div id="messages">
  <%= for msg <- @messages do %>
  <p><%= msg.sender %>: <%= msg.body %></p>
  <% end %>
  </div>
  <.form let={f} for={:message} phx-submit="new_msg">
  <%= text_input f, :message, value: @message, placeholder: "Enter message"%>
```

```
<%= submit "Send" %>
</.form>
</div>
</div>
<script>
window.addEventListener('phx:new_msg', (e) => {
let                    messagesContainer                    =
document.getElementById('messages');
let messageElement = document.createElement('p');
messageElement.textContent    =    `${e.detail.sender}:
${e.detail.body}`;
messagesContainer.appendChild(messageElement);
});
</script>
"""

end
end
```

10. **Update the layout:** Open **root.html.leex** and add this line within the **<head>** tag to enable Presence:

HTML

```
<script>window.userToken = "<%= assigns[:user_token] %>";</script>
```

11. **Update the router:** Open **router.ex** and add the following route:

Elixir

```
live "/chat", ChatLive, :index
```

12. **Start the server:**

Bash

```
mix phx.server
```

13. **Visit the page (in multiple browser windows):** Open your browser and go to http://localhost:4000/chat?user_name=Alice in one window and http://localhost:4000/chat?user_name=Bob in another. You should see a simple chat interface. Type messages and send them – they'll appear in both windows in real-time!

Explanation:

- **RoomChannel:** This channel handles users joining the "room:lobby" topic and broadcasting new messages to everyone in the room.[7]
- **Presence:** This module tracks which users are present in the channel.[8]
- **ChatLive:** This LiveView displays the chat messages and the list of online users.[9] It also handles sending new messages to the channel and updating the UI with new messages and presence updates.

This example demonstrates the basic principles of Channels and Presence. You can expand this to build more complex chat features like private messaging, typing indicators, and more.[1]

9.2 WebSockets and Phoenix PubSub

Under the hood, Phoenix Channels use WebSockets to provide the real-time communication layer. WebSockets are a communication protocol that enables persistent, bidirectional connections between clients and servers. your LiveView applications.

WebSockets:

Think of WebSockets as a persistent, two-way communication channel between your web browser and the server. Unlike traditional HTTP requests, which are short-lived and unidirectional, WebSockets allow for continuous data flow in both directions. This means that the server can push updates to the client without the client having to constantly poll for new information.

Why WebSockets are Awesome for Real-time Apps:

- **Low Latency:** WebSockets have very low latency, meaning messages are delivered almost instantly. This is crucial for applications where real-time updates are essential, like chat, games, or collaborative tools.
- **Efficient Communication:** WebSockets are more efficient than constantly polling the server for updates, reducing network overhead and server load.

- **Bi-directional Communication:** Both the client and the server can send messages at any time, enabling truly interactive experiences.

Phoenix PubSub: The Message Distributor

While WebSockets provide the connection, Phoenix PubSub acts as the message distributor. It's a powerful publish-subscribe system that allows different parts of your application (and even different servers) to communicate efficiently.

How PubSub Works:

1. **Publish:** When something interesting happens in your application (like a new chat message or a data update), the server *publishes* a message to a specific topic (like a channel name).
2. **Subscribe:** Clients that are interested in that topic *subscribe* to it.
3. **Distribute:** Phoenix PubSub efficiently distributes the message to all subscribed clients, regardless of which server they are connected to.

Why PubSub is Important for Scalability:

- **Handles Many Connections:** PubSub can handle a large number of concurrent connections and messages, making your real-time applications scalable.
- **Distributes Across Servers:** In a multi-server environment, PubSub ensures that messages are delivered to all subscribed clients, even if they are connected to different servers.

- **Decouples Components:** PubSub allows different parts of your application to communicate without being directly coupled, making your code more modular and maintainable.

Let's Get Practical: Building a Simple Broadcast System

Let's create a simple example to demonstrate how WebSockets and PubSub work together. We'll build a system that broadcasts a message to all connected clients.

1. **Create a new Phoenix project:**

Bash

```
mix phx.new my_pubsub_app
cd my_pubsub_app
```

2. **Create a Channel:**

Bash

```
mix phx.gen.channel Broadcast
```

3. **Update the Channel:** Open the generated broadcast_channel.ex file and update it:

Elixir

```
defmodule MyPubsubAppWeb.BroadcastChannel do
use MyPubsubAppWeb, :channel
def join("broadcast:global", _payload, socket) do
{:ok, socket}
```

```
end
def handle_in("shout", %{"message" => message},
socket) do
MyPubsubAppWeb.Endpoint.broadcast!("broadcast:global"
, "new_shout", %{message: message})
{:noreply, socket}
end
def handle_out("new_shout", payload, socket) do
push socket, "new_shout", payload
{:noreply, socket}
end
end
```

4. **Update the UserSocket:** Open **user_socket.ex** and add the channel route:

Elixir

```
## Channels
channel                                          "broadcast:*",
MyPubsubAppWeb.BroadcastChannel
```

5. **Create a LiveView:**

Bash

mix phx.gen.live Broadcast broadcast

6. **Update the LiveView:** Open the generated **broadcast_live.ex** file and update it:

Elixir

```elixir
defmodule MyPubsubAppWeb.BroadcastLive do
use MyPubsubAppWeb, :live_view
def mount(_params, _session, socket) do
if                   connected?(socket),                do:
MyPubsubAppWeb.Endpoint.subscribe("broadcast:global"
)
{:ok, assign(socket, message: "", shouts: [])}
end
def handle_event("shout", %{"message" => message},
socket) do

MyPubsubAppWeb.Endpoint.broadcast!("broadcast:global
", "shout", %{message: message})
{:noreply, assign(socket, message: "")}
end
def handle_info(%{event: "shout", payload: payload},
socket) do
{:noreply,    update(socket,    :shouts,    fn    shouts    ->
[payload.message | shouts] end)}
end

def render(assigns) do
~L"""
<h2>Shout!</h2>
<.form let={f} for={:message} phx-submit="shout">
<%= text_input f, :message, value: @message %>
<%= submit "Send" %>
</.form>

<h3>Shouts:</h3>
```

```
<ul id="shouts">
<%= for shout <- @shouts do %>
<li><%= shout %></li>
<% end %>
</ul>
"""
end
end
```

7. **Update the router:** Open **router.ex** and add the following route:

Elixir

live "/broadcast", BroadcastLive, :index

8. **Start the server:**

Bash

mix phx.server

9. **Visit the page (in multiple browser windows):** Open **http://localhost:4000/broadcast** in multiple browser windows. Type a message in one window and click "Send". The message will appear in all connected windows in real-time!

Explanation:

- **BroadcastChannel:** This channel handles broadcasting messages to the "broadcast:global" topic.
- **BroadcastLive:** This LiveView allows users to send messages and displays the received messages.
- **WebSockets:** The underlying WebSocket connection enables real-time communication between the clients and the server.
- **PubSub:** Phoenix PubSub distributes the messages to all subscribed clients.

This example demonstrates a simple broadcast system using WebSockets and PubSub. You can expand this to build more complex real-time features in your LiveView applications.

Chapter 10: Case Study: Building a Real-Time Dashboard

It's time to put all the skills you've learned to the test and build a real-world application! In this chapter, we'll walk through the process of creating a real-time dashboard using LiveView. This dashboard will display dynamic data that updates automatically, giving you a taste of how to build engaging and informative applications that respond to changes in real-time.

Our Dashboard: Visualizing Website Traffic

For this case study, we'll build a dashboard that visualizes website traffic data. Imagine you have a website, and you want to see how many visitors are currently online, which pages they are viewing, and how that traffic changes over time. This dashboard will give you that insight in a clear and dynamic way.

10.1 Project Setup and Planning

Before we jump headfirst into building our real-time dashboard, let's take a moment to plan things out! Just like a good architect wouldn't start building a skyscraper without blueprints, we need a solid plan for our project. This will help us stay organized, make informed decisions, and ensure we build a dashboard that meets our needs.

1. Define the Purpose and Scope

First things first, let's clarify what we want to achieve with our dashboard.

- **Purpose:** Our dashboard will visualize website traffic data in real-time, providing insights into visitor activity and trends.
- **Scope:** For this case study, we'll focus on key metrics like the number of online visitors, page views, and traffic trends over time.

2. Choose the Technology Stack

Next, let's select the tools we'll use to bring our dashboard to life. We'll stick with the technologies we've been exploring throughout this book:

- **Phoenix Framework:** This will be the foundation of our web application.

- **LiveView:** We'll use LiveView to build the dynamic and interactive dashboard interface.
- **Phoenix Channels:** We'll leverage Channels to push real-time updates to the dashboard.
- **Chart.js:** This JavaScript library will help us create visually appealing charts to display traffic trends.

3. Set Up the Project

With our purpose and tools defined, let's create a new Phoenix project to house our dashboard.

Bash

```
mix phx.new my_dashboard_app
cd my_dashboard_app
```

4. Plan the Data Source

In a real-world scenario, your dashboard would likely integrate with a database, a third-party analytics service, or other data sources to fetch real website traffic data. For this case study, we'll keep things simple and simulate the data. We'll create a process that generates random traffic data and pushes it to the dashboard in real-time.

5. Design the Dashboard Layout

Before writing any code, it's helpful to sketch out a rough layout for your dashboard. Think about how you want to present the information:

- **Metrics:** How will you display the key metrics (visitor count, page views)?

- **Charts:** What type of chart will best visualize the traffic trends?
- **Overall Structure:** How will you arrange the different elements on the dashboard for clarity and readability?

6. Consider User Experience (UX)

Think about the user's perspective:

- **Clarity:** Is the information presented in a clear and easy-to-understand way?
- **Responsiveness:** Does the dashboard adapt well to different screen sizes?
- **Interactivity:** Are there any interactive elements that would enhance the user's experience?

7. Plan for Scalability (Optional)

If you anticipate high traffic or a large number of concurrent users, consider how your dashboard will scale. This might involve:

- **Database Optimization:** Ensure your database can handle the expected load.
- **Caching:** Cache frequently accessed data to reduce database queries.
- **Horizontal Scaling:** Deploy your application across multiple servers to handle increased traffic.

By following these planning steps, you'll have a solid foundation for building your real-time dashboard. This careful preparation will help you make informed decisions throughout the development process and ensure your dashboard is efficient, user-friendly, and meets your goals.

10.2 Implementing Live Charts and Graphs

Let's make our dashboard visually appealing and informative by adding live charts and graphs! Charts are excellent for visualizing data and revealing trends that might not be immediately obvious from raw numbers.[1] In this section, we'll use Chart.js, a popular JavaScript library, to create a dynamic chart that updates in real-time with our website traffic data.[2]

Why Chart.js?

Chart.js is a great choice for our dashboard because it's:

- **Easy to Use:** It has a simple and intuitive API for creating various chart types.[3]
- **Flexible:** It offers a wide range of customization options to tailor the chart's appearance and behavior.[4]
- **Interactive:** It supports features like tooltips, zooming, and panning, allowing users to explore the data in more detail.[5]
- **Well-documented:** It has excellent documentation and a large community, making it easy to find answers and get help.[6]

Integrating Chart.js with LiveView

Here's how we'll integrate Chart.js with our LiveView dashboard:

1. **Install Chart.js:** We'll use npm to install Chart.js:

Bash

```
npm install chart.js
```

2. **Prepare the Data:** Our LiveView will need to prepare the data in a format that Chart.js can understand. This typically involves structuring the data as a JavaScript object with labels and datasets.
3. **Render the Chart:** We'll include a `<canvas>` element in our LiveView template where the chart will be rendered. We'll then use JavaScript within a `<script>` tag to initialize a new Chart.js chart with the data provided by the LiveView.
4. **Update the Chart:** As new traffic data comes in, we'll update the chart dynamically using LiveView's real-time capabilities.

Let's Get Practical: Building a Live Traffic Chart

Let's add a line chart to our DashboardLive that visualizes traffic trends over time.

1. **Update the LiveView:** Open the dashboard_live.ex file and update it as follows:

Elixir

```
defmodule MyDashboardAppWeb.DashboardLive do
use MyDashboardAppWeb, :live_view
def mount(_params, _session, socket) do
```

```elixir
                    if    connected?(socket),    do:
MyDashboardAppWeb.Endpoint.subscribe("traffic_updat
es")
{:ok,
socket
|> assign(
visitor_count: 0,
page_views: %{},
traffic_data: %{
labels: [],
datasets: [%{
label: "Visitors",
data: [],
fill: false,
borderColor: "rgb(75, 192, 192)",
tension: 0.1
}]
}
)}
end

def handle_info(%{event: "traffic_update", payload:
payload}, socket) do
{:noreply,
socket
|> assign(visitor_count: payload.visitor_count)
|> assign(page_views: payload.page_views)
|> update(:traffic_data, fn traffic_data ->
%{
traffic_data
| labels: traffic_data.labels ++ [payload.time],
datasets: [
```

```
%{
traffic__data.datasets |> List.first()
              | data: traffic__data.datasets |> List.first() |>
Map.get(:data) ++ [payload.visitor__count]
}
]
}
end)}
end

def render(assigns) do
~L"""
<h1>Website Traffic Dashboard</h1>
<div id="dashboard">
<div class="metric">
<h2>Visitors Online</h2>
<p><%= @visitor__count %></p>
</div>
<div class="metric">
<h2>Page Views</h2>
<ul>
<%= for {page, count} <- @page__views do %>
<li><%= page %>: <%= count %></li>
<% end %>
</ul>
</div>
<div class="chart">
<h2>Traffic Trends</h2>
<canvas id="trafficChart"></canvas>
<script>
```

```
var                            ctx                            =
document.getElementById('trafficChart').getContext('2d'
);
var myChart = new Chart(ctx, {
type: 'line',
data: <%= Jason.encode!(@traffic_data) %>,
options: {}
});
</script>
</div>
</div>
"""

end
end
```

In this updated code:

- We initialize **traffic_data** in the **mount** function with empty labels and a dataset for "Visitors."
- The **handle_info** function updates **traffic_data** with new labels (time) and data (visitor count) whenever a "traffic_update" event is received.
- The **render** function now includes a <canvas> element with the ID "trafficChart" and a <script> tag that initializes a new Chart.js line chart using the **@traffic_data** assign.

This setup will dynamically update the chart whenever new traffic data is pushed to the LiveView. We'll handle the data simulation and pushing updates in the next section.

10.3 Integrating with External APIs

Alright, it's time to bring our dashboard to life by feeding it some real-time data! In this section, we'll simulate website traffic data and push updates to our LiveView dashboard using Phoenix Channels. This will demonstrate how to integrate your dashboard with external sources of information, whether it's a database, a third-party analytics service, or any other system that provides data.

Simulating the Data:

Since we don't have a real website with live traffic data, we'll create a process that simulates this data. This process will generate random visitor counts and page view data at regular intervals and broadcast this data to our dashboard.

Using Phoenix Channels for Real-time Updates

We'll use Phoenix Channels to push these data updates to the dashboard in real-time.[1] This will allow the dashboard to react instantly to changes in the data, providing a truly dynamic and engaging experience.

Let's Get Practical:

1. **Create a GenServer:** Create a new file named traffic_simulator.ex in your lib/my_dashboard_app directory. This GenServer will be responsible for generating and broadcasting the traffic data.

Elixir

```
defmodule MyDashboardApp.TrafficSimulator do
```

```elixir
use GenServer
def start_link(opts) do
GenServer.start_link(__MODULE__,        opts,        name:
__MODULE__)
end
def init(opts) do
send(self(), :generate_traffic)
{:ok, opts}
end

def handle_info(:generate_traffic, state) do
# Simulate visitor count and page views
visitor_count = Enum.random(10..100)
page_views = %{
"/": Enum.random(1..50),
"/about": Enum.random(1..30),
"/contact": Enum.random(1..20)
}

# Broadcast the data

MyDashboardAppWeb.Endpoint.broadcast!("traffic_upda
tes", "traffic_update", %{
visitor_count: visitor_count,
page_views: page_views,
time:  DateTime.now("Etc/UTC")  |>  DateTime.to_time()
|> Time.to_string()
})
# Schedule the next traffic generation
Process.send_after(self(), :generate_traffic, 5000)
{:noreply, state}
end
```

end

2. This **TrafficSimulator** GenServer generates random visitor_count and page_views data every 5 seconds. It then broadcasts this data along with a timestamp to the "traffic_updates" topic using MyDashboardAppWeb.Endpoint.broadcast!.

3. **Start the GenServer:** To start this GenServer when your application starts, add it to your supervision tree in lib/my_dashboard_app/application.ex:

Elixir

```
def start(_type, _args) do
children = [
# ... other children ...
MyDashboardApp.TrafficSimulator
]
opts        =         [strategy:        :one_for_one,        name:
MyDashboardApp.Supervisor]
Supervisor.start_link(children, opts)
end
```

Connecting the Dashboard to the Data Stream

Now that we have our traffic data simulator, let's connect our DashboardLive to receive these real-time updates.

1. **Subscribe to the Topic:** In your DashboardLive module's **mount** function, subscribe to the "traffic_updates" topic:

Elixir

```elixir
def mount(_params, _session, socket) do
  if connected?(socket), do: MyDashboardAppWeb.Endpoint.subscribe("traffic_updates")
  # ... rest of your mount function ...
end
```

2. **Handle Incoming Data:** Add a `handle_info` function to your DashboardLive to handle the incoming traffic data:

Elixir

```elixir
def handle_info(%{event: "traffic_update", payload: payload}, socket) do
  {:noreply,
  socket
  |> assign(visitor_count: payload.visitor_count)
  |> assign(page_views: payload.page_views)
  |> update(:traffic_data, fn traffic_data ->
  %{
  traffic_data
  | labels: traffic_data.labels ++ [payload.time],
  datasets: [
  %{
  traffic_data.datasets |> List.first()
          | data: traffic_data.datasets |> List.first() |> Map.get(:data) ++ [payload.visitor_count]
  }
  ]
  }
  end)}
```

end

3. This function updates the **visitor_count**, **page_views**, and **traffic_data** assigns with the received data.

Running the Dashboard

Now, when you run your Phoenix application (**mix phx.server**) and visit **/dashboard** in your browser, you should see a live dashboard that updates every 5 seconds with the simulated traffic data! The chart will dynamically reflect the changes in visitor count over time.

This example demonstrates how to integrate your LiveView dashboard with an external API (in this case, our simulated traffic data). You can adapt this approach to connect to various data sources and create dynamic, real-time dashboards that visualize information in an engaging and informative way.

Chapter 11: Building an Interactive Game

Get ready to level up your LiveView skills by building an interactive game! This case study will take you beyond dashboards and forms, showing you how to create engaging, real-time gaming experiences with the power of Elixir and LiveView. We'll combine the concepts we've learned so far, including state management, event handling, and real-time updates, to build a game that's both fun and educational.

Our Game:

For this case study, we'll create a simple number guessing game. The game will generate a random secret number, and the player needs to guess it within a certain number of attempts. We'll provide feedback to the player after each guess, guiding them towards the correct answer.

11.1 Game Design and Logic

Alright, before we start coding our number guessing game, let's put on our game designer hats and think about how the game should work! A well-defined game design is like a solid blueprint – it guides your development process and ensures a fun and engaging experience for the players.

Core Mechanics:

Let's define the core mechanics of our number guessing game:

- **The Secret Number:** The game will generate a random secret number between 1 and 100. This will be the number the player needs to guess.
- **Limited Attempts:** To add a bit of challenge, the player will have a limited number of attempts to guess the number. Let's give them 10 attempts.
- **Feedback:** After each guess, the game will provide feedback to the player, letting them know if their guess was too high, too low, or correct. This feedback is crucial for guiding the player towards the correct answer.

Game State:

To manage the game's flow and logic, we'll need to keep track of various pieces of information. This is our game state:

- secret_number: This stores the randomly generated secret number.
- attempts_left: This keeps track of how many attempts the player has remaining.
- current_guess: This stores the player's current guess.
- feedback: This holds the feedback message to be displayed to the player (e.g., "Too high!", "Too low!", or "Correct!").
- game_over: This is a boolean value that indicates whether the game is over (either the player guessed correctly or ran out of attempts).

Game Flow:

Let's outline the step-by-step flow of our game:

1. **Initialization:** When the game starts, we generate a random secret_number and set attempts_left to 10. The other state variables (current_guess, feedback, and game_over) are initialized to their default values.
2. **Guessing:** The player enters their guess through a form.
3. **Evaluation:** When the player submits their guess, we compare it to the secret_number.
   - If the guess is correct, we update the feedback to "Correct!" and set game_over to true.
   - If the guess is higher than the secret_number, we update the feedback to "Too high!".
   - If the guess is lower than the secret_number, we update the feedback to "Too low!".
4. **Decrement Attempts:** We decrement the attempts_left counter.
5. **Game Over Check:** We check if the game is over:
   - If the guess was correct or attempts_left has reached 0, the game is over. We display the secret_number and a "Play Again" button.
   - Otherwise, the game continues, and the player can make another guess.

Let's Get Practical:

We'll implement this game logic in a LiveView shortly. For now, let's see how we can initialize the game state in the mount function of our LiveView:

Elixir

```elixir
defmodule MyDashboardAppWeb.NumberGuessingLive do
use MyDashboardAppWeb, :live_view
def mount(_params, _session, socket) do
{:ok,
socket
|> assign(
secret_number: Enum.random(1..100),
attempts_left: 10,
current_guess: nil,
feedback: nil,
game_over: false
)}
end
# ... rest of the LiveView code ...
end
```

This **mount** function sets up the initial state of our game with a random **secret_number** and 10 attempts. We'll implement the rest of the game logic in the following sections.

11.2 Handling User Input and Game State

Now that we have the game design and logic figured out, let's bring our number guessing game to life with LiveView! This section will focus on handling user input, updating the game state, and providing feedback to the player.

Creating the LiveView Structure

First, let's generate a new LiveView module for our game.

1. **Generate the LiveView:** In your terminal, run the following command:

Bash

```
mix phx.gen.live NumberGuessing number_guessing
```

2. This will create a **NumberGuessingLive** module and its corresponding template file.
3. **Update the LiveView:** Open the generated number_guessing_live.ex file and replace its contents with the following code:

Elixir

```
defmodule MyDashboardAppWeb.NumberGuessingLive do
use MyDashboardAppWeb, :live_view
def mount(_params, _session, socket) do
{:ok,
socket
|> assign(
secret_number: Enum.random(1..100),
attempts_left: 10,
current_guess: nil,
feedback: nil,
game_over: false
)}
end
def handle_event("guess", %{"guess" => guess}, socket)
do
```

```elixir
guess = String.to_integer(guess)
attempts_left = socket.assigns.attempts_left - 1
cond do
guess == socket.assigns.secret_number ->
{:noreply,
socket
|> assign(current_guess: guess, feedback: "Correct!",
game_over: true, attempts_left: attempts_left)}

guess > socket.assigns.secret_number ->
{:noreply,
socket
|> assign(current_guess: guess, feedback: "Too high!",
attempts_left: attempts_left)}
guess < socket.assigns.secret_number ->
{:noreply,
socket
|> assign(current_guess: guess, feedback: "Too low!",
attempts_left: attempts_left)}
end
end

def render(assigns) do
~L"""
<h1>Number Guessing Game</h1>
<div id="game">
<%= if @game_over do %>
<h2>Game Over!</h2>
<p>The number was <%= @secret_number %></p>
                <%= live_patch "Play Again", to:
Routes.number_guessing_path(@socket, :index) %>
<% else %>
```

```
<p>I'm thinking of a number between 1 and 100.</p>
<p>You have <%= @attempts_left %> attempts left.</p>
<%= if @feedback do %>
<p><%= @feedback %></p>
<% end %>
<.form let={f} for={:guess} phx-submit="guess">
<%= number_input f, :guess, min: 1, max: 100 %>
<%= submit "Guess" %>
</.form>
<% end %>
</div>
"""

end
end
```

4. **Update the router:** Open your **router.ex** file and add the following route within the **scope "/",** **MyDashboardAppWeb** block:

Elixir

```
live "/number_guessing", NumberGuessingLive, :index
```

Handling User Input: The handle_event Function

The handle_event function is where the magic happens. It's responsible for:

- Receiving the player's guess from the form submission.
- Comparing the guess to the secret number.
- Providing feedback to the player.

- Updating the game state.

In our **handle_event** function:

- We extract the **guess** from the submitted form data.
- We convert the **guess** to an integer using **String.to_integer(guess)**.
- We decrement the **attempts_left** counter.
- We use a **cond** statement to check if the guess is correct, too high, or too low, and provide the appropriate feedback.
- We update the socket's assigns with the **current_guess**, feedback, **game_over** status, and **attempts_left**.

Rendering the Game: The render Function

The **render** function displays the game interface to the player. It uses conditional rendering to show different content based on the game state:

- If **game_over** is **true**, it displays the "Game Over!" message along with the **secret_number** and a "Play Again" button.
- If **game_over** is **false**, it shows the instructions, the number of **attempts_left**, the **feedback** (if any), and the form for the player to enter their guess.

Running the Game

Now, if you start your Phoenix server (**mix phx.server**) and visit /number_guessing in your browser, you can play the number guessing game! Try entering different guesses and see how the game provides feedback and updates the state accordingly.

This section demonstrates how to handle user input, manage game state, and provide feedback in a LiveView application. By combining these concepts, you can create engaging and interactive games that respond to the player's actions in real-time.

11.3 Creating Animations and Visual Effects

Let's add some visual flair to our number guessing game! While the game is functional, a few animations and visual effects can make it more engaging and enjoyable for the player. In this section, we'll explore how to use JavaScript and CSS to enhance the game's presentation.

Why Animations and Visual Effects?

Animations and visual effects can significantly improve the user experience by:

- **Providing Feedback:** Animations can provide visual cues to the player, confirming their actions and making the interface feel more responsive.
- **Enhancing Engagement:** Visual effects can add a sense of excitement and dynamism to the game, keeping the player more engaged.
- **Improving Aesthetics:** Well-designed animations can make the game more visually appealing and polished.

Our Animation: Highlighting the Feedback

For our number guessing game, we'll add a simple animation that highlights the feedback message when it's updated. This will draw the player's attention to the feedback and make it more noticeable.

Let's Get Practical: Adding the Animation

1. **Add JavaScript to the LiveView:** We'll use JavaScript to add a CSS class to the feedback element when it's updated. This CSS class will trigger the animation. Update your render function in number_guessing_live.ex as follows:

Elixir

```
def render(assigns) do
~L"""
<h1>Number Guessing Game</h1>
<div id="game">
<%= if @game_over do %>
<h2>Game Over!</h2>
<p>The number was <%= @secret_number %></p>
            <%= live_patch "Play Again", to:
Routes.number_guessing_path(@socket, :index) %>
<% else %>
<p>I'm thinking of a number between 1 and 100.</p>
<p>You have <%= @attempts_left %> attempts left.</p>
<%= if @feedback do %>
<p><%= @feedback %></p>
<% end %>
<.form let={f} for={:guess} phx-submit="guess">
<%= number_input f, :guess, min: 1, max: 100 %>
<%= submit "Guess" %>
</.form>
<% end %>
```

```
</div>
<script>
window.addEventListener('phx:feedback', (e) => {
let feedbackElement = document.querySelector('#game
p:last-of-type');
feedbackElement.classList.add('highlight');
setTimeout(() => {
feedbackElement.classList.remove('highlight');
}, 1000);
});
</script>
"""
```

end

2. This script listens for a custom "phx:feedback" event that we'll push from the LiveView. When this event is received, it selects the last `<p>` tag within the **#game** element (which is our feedback message), adds the **highlight** class to it, and then removes the class after 1 second (1000 milliseconds).

3. **Add CSS for the Animation:** In your **assets/css/app.css** file, add the following CSS code:

CSS

```
.highlight {
animation: feedback-highlight 1s ease;
}
@keyframes feedback-highlight {
0% { background-color: yellow; }
100% { background-color: transparent; }
}
```

4. This CSS creates an animation called **feedback-highlight** that smoothly transitions the background color of the element from yellow to transparent over 1 second.

5. **Trigger the Animation:** Now, we need to trigger this animation from our LiveView. In your **handle_event** function, push a "feedback" event after providing feedback to the player:

Elixir

```elixir
def handle_event("guess", %{"guess" => guess}, socket)
do
# ... existing code ...
{:noreply,
socket
|> assign(current_guess: guess, feedback: feedback,
attempts_left: attempts_left)
|> push_event("feedback", %{})}
end
```

6. This code pushes a "feedback" event to the client whenever the **handle_event** function is called for a "guess" event. This will trigger the JavaScript code we added in step 1 to apply the animation.

Running the Game with Animation

Now, if you start your Phoenix server and play the number guessing game, you'll see that the feedback message is briefly highlighted in yellow after each guess! This simple

174

animation provides a visual cue to the player, acknowledging their input and making the game feel more responsive.

This example demonstrates how to add animations and visual effects to your LiveView applications using JavaScript and CSS. You can use this approach to create a wide range of animations and effects, enhancing the user experience and making your applications more engaging.

Chapter 12: Deployment and Beyond

You've built an amazing LiveView application! Now it's time to share it with the world. This chapter covers the essential aspects of deploying your Phoenix application, ensuring it runs smoothly in a production environment, and continuing to improve its performance and reliability over time.

12.1 Deploying Phoenix Applications

Alright, you've poured your heart and soul into building an amazing LiveView application! Now it's time to set it free and share it with the world. This involves deploying your application, which essentially means making it accessible to users on the internet. Think of it as launching your spaceship into orbit after meticulously building it in your garage.

Choosing Your Launchpad:

Just like a spaceship needs a launchpad, your application needs a place to live on the internet. There are various hosting providers that cater to Phoenix applications, each with its own strengths and tradeoffs.

- **Elixir-Specific Platforms:** These platforms are like specialized launchpads designed specifically for Elixir rockets. They offer streamlined deployment processes, optimized environments, and often come with Elixir-savvy support. Some popular options include:

- **Gigalixir:** Known for its simplicity and ease of use, especially for beginners.
- **Fly.io:** Offers a global presence with servers in multiple regions, great for low-latency applications.
- **Render:** Provides a smooth deployment experience and integrates well with GitHub for automated deployments.
- **Cloud Providers:** These are like giant space stations that can accommodate all sorts of applications, including your Phoenix app. They offer flexibility, scalability, and a wide range of services. Some popular cloud providers include:
  - **AWS (Amazon Web Services):** The industry giant with a vast array of services and global infrastructure.
  - **Google Cloud Platform (GCP):** Google's cloud offering, known for its strong focus on data analytics and machine learning.
  - **Azure:** Microsoft's cloud platform, often favored by enterprises with existing Microsoft infrastructure.
- **VPS (Virtual Private Server):** This is like having your own private spaceship. You rent a virtual server and have full control over its configuration. This gives you maximum flexibility but also requires more technical expertise to manage the server environment.

Preparing for Launch: Pre-Deployment Checklist

Before deploying your application, there are a few crucial steps to take:

1. **Configure Environment Variables:** Your production environment will likely have different settings than your development environment. You'll need to configure environment variables for things like database credentials, API keys, and other sensitive information.
2. **Compile Assets:** Phoenix uses Webpack to manage your frontend assets (JavaScript, CSS, etc.). You'll need to compile these assets for production to optimize their size and performance. You can do this by running:

Bash

mix assets.deploy

3. **Create a Release:** Phoenix provides a mechanism to create a self-contained release of your application. This bundles your application code and its dependencies into a single package that can be easily deployed to your server. You can create a release by running:

Bash

mix release

Launching Your Application:

The specific deployment steps will vary depending on your chosen hosting provider. However, the general process typically involves:

1. **Server Setup:** If you're not using an Elixir-specific platform, you'll need to set up a server environment. This might involve creating a server instance on a cloud provider or configuring a VPS. You'll also need to install Elixir and any required dependencies on the server.
2. **Upload Your Release:** Upload the release package you created to your server.
3. **Start the Application:** Use the release's start script to start your Phoenix application on the server.
4. **Configure Web Server:** You'll likely need to configure a web server (like Nginx or Cowboy) to act as a reverse proxy, handling incoming requests and forwarding them to your Phoenix application.
5. **Configure Domain Name:** If you have a domain name, you'll need to configure its DNS settings to point to your server's IP address.

Example: Deploying to Gigalixir

Gigalixir is known for its straightforward deployment process. Here's a simplified example:

1. **Install the Gigalixir CLI:**

Bash

```
mix archive.install hex gigalixir
```

2. **Create a Gigalixir account and log in:**

Bash

```
gigalixir signup
gigalixir login
```

3. **Create a new app on Gigalixir:**

Bash

```
gigalixir create -s MIX_ENV=prod
```

4. **Set up a database:**

Bash

```
gigalixir pg:create
```

5. **Deploy your application:**

Bash

```
gigalixir deploy
```

Gigalixir takes care of much of the server configuration and deployment process, making it easy to get your Phoenix application up and running.

Exploring Other Deployment Options

This section provides a general overview of deploying Phoenix applications. For more detailed instructions and specific guides for different hosting providers, refer to the official Phoenix documentation and the documentation of your chosen platform.

12.2 Continuous Integration and Delivery

Let's talk about how to streamline your development process and deliver high-quality applications with Continuous Integration and Delivery (CI/CD)! Think of CI/CD as an automated pipeline that takes your code from your local machine to your users' hands with minimal manual intervention. It's like having a dedicated team of robots that build, test, and deploy your application whenever you make changes.

Why CI/CD? The Benefits of Automation

CI/CD brings a number of advantages to your development workflow:

- **Catch Bugs Early:** Automated tests run on every code change, catching bugs and issues before they reach your users. This saves you time and headaches in the long run.
- **Deploy Frequently:** CI/CD makes it easy to deploy new features and updates frequently, allowing you to deliver value to your users faster and get feedback more quickly.
- **Reduce Errors:** Automation minimizes the risk of human error in the deployment process, ensuring consistency and reliability.

- **Improve Collaboration:** CI/CD encourages better collaboration among developers by providing a shared and transparent workflow.
- **Increase Confidence:** Knowing that your code is constantly being tested and deployed gives you greater confidence in its quality and stability.

The CI/CD Pipeline: A Step-by-Step Journey

A typical CI/CD pipeline for a Phoenix application might look like this:

1. **Code Changes:** A developer writes code and commits it to a version control system like Git.
2. **Build:** The CI/CD system detects the code changes and triggers a build process. This might involve compiling the code, running database migrations, and building assets.
3. **Test:** Automated tests are run to ensure the code changes haven't introduced any bugs or regressions. This might include unit tests, integration tests, and end-to-end tests.
4. **Deploy to Staging:** If the build and tests pass, the application is automatically deployed to a staging environment. This is a pre-production environment that closely resembles the live production environment.
5. **Testing in Staging:** Manual or automated tests can be performed in the staging environment to further validate the changes before they go live.
6. **Deploy to Production:** Once the staging deployment is approved, the application is deployed to the

production environment, making the new features or updates available to users.

Choosing Your CI/CD Tools

There are various CI/CD tools available, each with its own strengths and features. Some popular options include:

- **GitHub Actions:** Tightly integrated with GitHub, making it convenient for projects hosted on GitHub. It offers a wide range of pre-built actions and allows you to define custom workflows.
- **CircleCI:** A cloud-based CI/CD platform that supports various languages and frameworks, including Elixir and Phoenix. It offers a flexible and scalable solution for automating your builds and deployments.
- **GitLab CI/CD:** Built into GitLab, providing a comprehensive CI/CD solution within the GitLab ecosystem. It offers features like continuous integration, continuous delivery, and continuous deployment.

Let's Get Practical: Setting Up a CI/CD Pipeline with GitHub Actions

Let's walk through a basic example of setting up a CI/CD pipeline with GitHub Actions for a Phoenix application.

1. **Create a Workflow File:** In your Phoenix project, create a directory named .github/workflows at the root of your project. Inside this directory, create a file named ci.yml. This file will define your CI/CD workflow.
2. **Define the Workflow:** Add the following code to your ci.yml file:

3. YAML

```yaml
name: CI

on:
push:
branches: [ main ]
pull_request:
branches: [ main ]

jobs:
build:
runs-on: ubuntu-latest

steps:
- uses: actions/checkout@v3
- name:¹ Set up Elixir
uses: actions/setup-elixir@v2
with:
elixir-version: '1.14' # Replace with your desired Elixir version
- name: Install dependencies
run: mix deps.get
- name: Run tests
run: mix test
```

4. This workflow file defines a job named "build" that runs on the latest Ubuntu environment. It checks out your code, sets up Elixir, installs dependencies, and runs your tests.
5. **Push to GitHub:** Commit and push this workflow file to your GitHub repository.

Now, whenever you push code changes to your main branch, GitHub Actions will automatically run this workflow, building your application and running your tests. This is a basic example, and you can expand it to include deployment steps, database migrations, and other tasks in your CI/CD pipeline.

By implementing CI/CD, you can automate your development process, improve code quality, and deliver value to your users more efficiently.

12.3 Performance Monitoring and Optimization

You've deployed your Phoenix application and it's live! But the journey doesn't end there. To ensure your application remains fast, efficient, and reliable, you need to keep an eye on its performance and optimize it over time. Think of it like keeping your spaceship running smoothly after launch – regular checkups and maintenance are essential for a successful mission.

Why Monitor and Optimize?

Performance monitoring and optimization are crucial for several reasons:

- **User Experience:** A slow or unresponsive application can frustrate users and drive them away. Monitoring helps you identify and address performance bottlenecks that might be affecting the user experience.

- **Resource Efficiency:** Optimizing your application can reduce resource usage (CPU, memory, bandwidth), potentially saving you money on hosting costs.
- **Scalability:** As your application grows and handles more traffic, performance optimization becomes even more critical to ensure it can scale effectively.
- **Stability:** Monitoring can help you detect and diagnose errors or issues that might be affecting your application's stability and uptime.

Monitoring Tools: Keeping an Eye on Your App

There are various tools available to help you monitor your Phoenix application's performance:

- **LiveDashboard:** Phoenix comes with a built-in LiveDashboard that provides real-time insights into your application's performance. It shows metrics like request latency, memory usage, and process distribution. You can access it by visiting /dashboard in your running application.
- **Observer:** Erlang's Observer tool allows you to inspect the state of your application's processes, memory usage, and other system metrics. You can start it by running :observer.start() in an IEx shell.
- **Third-Party Services:** Services like New Relic, Datadog, and AppSignal offer comprehensive performance monitoring, including application performance monitoring (APM), infrastructure monitoring, and error tracking.

Optimization Techniques: Fine-tuning Your App

Once you've identified potential performance bottlenecks through monitoring, you can apply various optimization techniques:

- **Database Optimization:**
  - **Efficient Queries:** Use Ecto's query functions effectively to avoid fetching unnecessary data.
  - **Indexes:** Add indexes to your database tables to speed up queries.
  - **Data Types:** Use appropriate data types for your database columns to optimize storage and retrieval.
- **Code Optimization:**
  - **Profiling:** Use profiling tools to identify performance hotspots in your code.
  - **Algorithm Efficiency:** Choose efficient algorithms and data structures.
  - **Code Refactoring:** Refactor code to reduce complexity and improve performance.
- **Caching:**
  - **ETS:** Use Erlang Term Storage (ETS) to cache frequently accessed data in memory.
  - **Phoenix.PubSub:** Leverage Phoenix.PubSub for caching data that needs to be shared across multiple processes.
- **Scaling:**
  - **Horizontal Scaling:** Add more servers to your application to handle increased traffic.
  - **Vertical Scaling:** Increase the resources (CPU, memory) of your existing servers.

Let's Get Practical: Using LiveDashboard

Let's explore how to use LiveDashboard to monitor your Phoenix application's performance.

1. **Start your application:** Run your Phoenix application with mix phx.server.
2. **Access LiveDashboard:** Open your browser and visit /dashboard.
3. **Explore the Metrics:** LiveDashboard provides various tabs with real-time metrics:
   - **System:** Shows overall system metrics like CPU usage, memory usage, and load average.
   - **Processes:** Displays information about the running processes in your application.
   - **Request:** Shows metrics related to HTTP requests, such as latency and request rate.
   - **Ecto:** Provides insights into database performance, including query times and connection pool usage.

By regularly monitoring these metrics, you can identify potential performance issues and take steps to optimize your application.

Continuous Optimization: An Ongoing Process

Performance optimization is an ongoing process. As your application grows and usage patterns change, you'll need to continue monitoring and adapting your optimization strategies. Regularly review your monitoring data, identify bottlenecks, and apply appropriate optimization techniques to ensure your Phoenix application remains fast, efficient, and provides a great experience for your users.

Conclusion

Congratulations, intrepid explorer! You've reached the end of this book, and along the way, you've ventured beyond the familiar territory of the backend to discover the exciting possibilities of frontend development with Elixir.

We started with the foundations of HTML, CSS, and JavaScript, laying the groundwork for building any web application. Then, we delved into the heart of Elixir web development with the Phoenix framework, uncovering its elegant structure and powerful features. But the real magic began when we unlocked the potential of LiveView, Elixir's secret weapon for crafting dynamic, real-time user interfaces.

You've learned how to build everything from simple interactive elements to complex, real-time applications, all while staying within the comfortable embrace of Elixir. We've explored how to integrate JavaScript libraries, build hybrid applications with frontend frameworks, and even create real-time communication features using Phoenix Channels.

But this is just the beginning! The world of frontend development with Elixir is constantly evolving, with new tools and techniques emerging all the time. As you continue your journey, remember to:

- **Embrace the LiveView philosophy:** Leverage the power of server-side rendering and state management to build efficient and maintainable applications.

- **Explore the Elixir ecosystem:** Discover new libraries and frameworks that can enhance your development workflow and expand your creative possibilities.
- **Stay curious and keep learning:** The web development landscape is constantly changing, so embrace continuous learning and experimentation.
- **Share your knowledge and contribute:** Join the vibrant Elixir community, share your experiences, and contribute to the growth of this amazing ecosystem.

Now, armed with the knowledge and skills you've gained from this book, go forth and build amazing things! Create web applications that are not only functional and performant but also delightful and engaging for your users. The future of frontend development with Elixir is bright, and you are now a part of it. Happy coding!

www.ingramcontent.com/pod-product-compliance
Lightning Source LLC
LaVergne TN
LVHW012334060326
832902LV00012B/1887